MORE THAN JUST A PLANT

MORE THAN JUST A PLANT

How to Care for Your Plants as They Care for You

KRYSTAL DURAN

COOL SPRINGS PRESS

Quarto.com

First Published in 2027 by Cool Springs Press, an imprint of The Quarto Group, 100 Cummings Center, Suite 265-D, Beverly, MA 01915, USA.
T (978) 282-9590 F (978) 283-2742

EEA Representation, WTS Tax d.o.o., Žanova ulica 3, 4000 Kranj, Slovenia.
www.wts-tax.si

31 30 29 28 27 1 2 3 4 5

ISBN: 978-1-57715-809-7

Digital edition published in 2027
eISBN: 978-1-57715-810-3

Library of Congress Cataloging-in-Publication Data
Names: Duran, Krystal, author.
Title: More than just a plant : how to care for your plants as they care for you / Krystal Duran.
Description: Beverly, MA : Cool Springs Press, 2026. | Includes index.
Identifiers: LCCN 2026017205 (print) | LCCN 2026017206 (ebook) | ISBN 9781577715809 (hardcover) | ISBN 9781577158103 (ebook)
Subjects: LCSH: House plants. | Indoor gardening.
Classification: LCC SB419 (print) | LCC SB419 (ebook)
LC record available at https://lccn.loc.gov/2026017205
LC ebook record available at https://lccn.loc.gov/

Design and page layout: Kelley Galbreath
Illustration: Esme Linton
Photography: Kat Schleicher, except Krystal Duran on pages 39 (bottom), 162, and 174

Printed in Guangdong, China TT072026

For anyone who thought
they were just buying
a plant and ended up
finding something more

contents

far left Even though I buy plants as houseplants, I choose to grow many of my bright-loving plants outside in pots on my covered porch during the spring and summer for ample growth. Shown here are my varieties of rubber tree plant (*Ficus elastica*).

left *Monstera deliciosa*, the statement plant that takes up the majority of space in my living room, is a constant reminder of how time and patience can grow incredible-sized leaves.

Introduction

"Why buy houseplants when they don't do anything for us? You can't eat them and it's time consuming to have to take care of them when they give us nothing in return. You should grow food instead."

I've read comments like these time and time again and if you're not a houseplant lover, you might ask this same question. I can assure you though that if you are a houseplant lover, and most likely that's why you are here reading this now, it's not a one-sided relationship. Sure, they can't audibly communicate with us, but plants have a way of speaking to us anyway. It's not in the ways we expect though. When we watch closely, they speak in gestures: the leaves reaching toward the light, plant tendrils forming to show us that they're looking for support, yellowing leaves falling to make space for more, and the new growth validating our patience and understanding of their silent cues.

I don't have much window space for plants so I grow the majority of my collection under grow lights. Grow lights give me the freedom to place plants where they feel right, not just where the sun happens to hit.

I know you're not going to tell me that an unfurling new leaf on your houseplant didn't make you squeal and jump for joy when you saw it, because no one has ever been unhappy seeing a new leaf unfurl . . . just saying. That part of plant collecting will always be just as exciting as the first time and it offers quite the boost of serotonin, no matter how many houseplants you grow. And don't get me started on new blooms on a plant! That will give you bragging rights for the rest of your life.

above, from left My outdoor garden is for the spring and summer, but my houseplants are for growing all year round.

Pablo, my mini Schnoodle, is my partner in crime in all my plant endeavors. Whether I'm repotting, watering, or rearranging plants for the hundredth time, he is always nearby, quietly observing, a constant presence in my plant care routine.

As plant lovers, we understand that even the smallest growth is something worth celebrating. Our plants are our own little individual teachers and companions. Plants connect us to people in our community and our loved ones. They keep us on our toes and can frustrate us to heck when we can't figure out what they want from us. But even then, we love them so.

I didn't quite understand the power of plants when I first started collecting. I knew I enjoyed them, I wanted more of them, and it was a hobby that quieted my brain during the hustle and bustle of the day. Over the years, though, and through my own loss, I realized these green babies are not only taking up every single empty space on my shelves, but they are also helping me heal. For that I will forever be grateful. So sure, houseplants may not be everyone's cup of tea, but if there's one thing I know about plants, it's that the relationship we have with them is very special. They are always *More Than Just a Plant*.

Oh, and by the way, I do grow food too!

1

Finding Peace Through Plants

I wasn't born with bright "green thumbs." In my mind, if I stared at a plant for too long, it would die. To some extent, that statement was absolutely true. I bought various plants, one of them being a majesty palm (*Ravenea rivularis*), which, looking back, was a huge red flag in the first place. If you know nothing about them, look at where they live in nature. Even in their natural environment (humid climates) their foliage has crispy tips. You'll find their fronds scattered all across the ground. In our homes, that is definitely reflected. Mine didn't last long.

When I first started growing houseplants, I placed plants in places so far away from windows they never stood a chance. I treated them like a piece of furniture and placed them in spots in my home that I *thought* looked good, versus really taking the time to learn about their proper care and providing them with the lighting requirements they needed. I ignored them until they were dry and brittle, and only attended to them long enough to hurl them into the dumpster.

One thing I had, though, was curiosity and an appreciation for plants from afar (and maybe a little stubbornness, too). I'm a girl happiest when I am among nature, and I hated not knowing how to take care of my plants well enough for them to thrive in my care. I've always been very inquisitive by nature, so having a hobby that allowed me to experiment was right up my alley. That didn't officially translate to action, though, until I bought my first cactus many years ago. Using hobbies to help guide us through life has always been true to my heart (and my psychology degree). Mindfulness was

a core practice in the work I did with youth. I trained and facilitated the work of managing aggressive behavior, and in the curriculum, it included therapeutically utilizing hobbies that fell into four subcategories: creative, physical, mindful, and social. I knew the importance of hobbies, but I also needed more of them myself.

While working with special needs youth in my community, I longed for a hobby to help me dive into my most mindful self. I have always enjoyed working with my hands, so I decided to give caring for plant life another go, and I soon fell deep into learning about plants and collecting them. Back when I started, though, I never believed that this hobby would pull me out of the darkest moments of my life. I, like many others,

below Finding ways to bring elements of nature into the workplace can be a way to practice mindfulness in a busy environment.

opposite A Chinese evergreen (*Aglaonema commutatum*) nicknamed Avatar was my late-husband's favorite plant. Although it suffered from root rot after his passing, Avatar—with the removal of the rot and consistent care—continues to be a part of my plant collection.

began sharing my love for plants on social media during the COVID-19 pandemic. I was searching for an online community of other plant lovers since I knew no one personally who enjoyed plants like I did.

No one in my "real life" cared about the tomatoes growing in my small garden or even batted an eye when I shared the joy of a new leaf unfurling. I was scrolling on Facebook Marketplace and found a local houseplant group where they shared the usernames of their plant accounts on other social media platforms. They shared their latest plant hauls and added pictures of their newest growth. I decided to create my own plant page and do the same.

I posted funny plant videos here and there. It was relatable to others who were going through similar experiences while building their own plant collections. I started to sprinkle in plant care tips along the way and continued to gain a dedicated community from there. When I was first starting, I found it very difficult to follow along at times because of the terminology used. I was extremely intimidated and had the fear I'd "mess" something up. I went into the world of providing plant care advice feeling a lot of pressure to succeed, versus learning through experimentation. I knew with my background in teaching and facilitating, I was most successful in giving information to others when I broke down complex ideas into smaller, simpler ones, in a way that everyone could understand. By doing so, it allowed me to reach people of all walks of life. I would like to say that this has been my superpower in the world of plants, and I take a lot of pride knowing that I now help a lot of people.

Little did I know that the decisions I made back then would change the entire trajectory of my life in more ways than I could ever describe. Aside from the world of plants, I wore many hats, and one of my hats was being a wife. I incorporated my husband in a few of my plant skits, and he played a huge role in helping me behind the scenes by making sure I was in the frame of the camera or giving me pointers on my editing. He was supportive of my journey with plants and teaching because he knew my passion for it and how fulfilled it made me.

When everything in life felt as though it was going better than I could even imagine, life decided to rewire things. I was married in 2010, and in 2022, I was suddenly widowed. Prior to my husband's passing, I had over 300 houseplants that I grew and loved. After he was gone, and because of my own depression, within the span of a few months, almost all of them were dead.

I was completely devastated in every way possible.

Turning Grief into Growth

Describing the pain of loss is something I don't think I'll ever know how to put into words. It was as if I was outside myself floating with nowhere to land. That pain physically hurts every part of the body, but yet at the same time, I felt so numb. The only thing that would make it better was to have my person back, and I found myself waiting by the door hoping it was just some horrible joke, and he'd come right back. Unfortunately, that never happened. How am I supposed to function after something like this? I can't physically get up to take care of myself, let alone care for anything else right now. And so I didn't. My occupation in the years leading up to my husband's death revolved around caring for others, and three months after my loss, I made the difficult decision to leave my position. And being a houseplant educator and enthusiast online, I'm supposed to have this well-kept collection, but my life had now fallen apart. How do I continue to show up? Do I even want to continue with these plants when nothing feels like it matters anymore? I was not okay and anyone who knows me knows that I am not a good faker, so showing up online and acting as if everything was fine was not an option for me. My emotions can be read all over my face.

There were mornings when I'd find myself sitting on the floor, surrounded by pots and soil, completely overwhelmed. Picking up one plant long enough to water it felt like moving a ton of bricks. I was broken, but what was left of my plant collection needed to be cared for. I tackled one plant at a time. Some I lost, but others held on. It gave me a reason to get up, even if it meant all the energy I had was just enough to throw one wilted plant away or water another. Other moments, my hands would be covered in soil, music softly playing in the background, the breeze coming through an open window, and it felt like grounding in the truest sense. These were moments of peace that I lacked for so long as I got lost in the care of my plants. One day at a time, one plant at a time.

The seconds without him eventually turned into minutes and minutes turned into hours. Hours turned to days and, before I knew it, time was passing . . . and I was actually surviving. Grief still showed up at my door, of course. Even now it still does, and it will always be there. Healing isn't linear, but my plants taught me how to make room for both growth

Observing the shape, color, texture, and new growth of foliage is a moment of escape from the noise.

and stillness. Some days I'd water and prune; other days, I'd just sit quietly beside them and let the silence be enough. What I know now that I didn't know then was that there is beauty in the growth after loss. Showing up online and rescuing my plants was a physical representation of rescuing myself and materializing what I had left after loss.

When the World Feels Heavy, Plants Are the Escape

When I shared my story, I was met with condolences and with words of encouragement. It was something I never would have anticipated. It opened up the conversation with others in my community about loss. I received messages with personal stories about grief. Although these stories initially were very overwhelming to this body that hadn't yet processed her own loss, it made me feel less alone. I shared the progression of my life through the world of plants and how much of an impact they made for me, and I continued to read others' stories. I realized that others have also longed for an outlet during their struggles with loss and mental health setbacks. Others were in very difficult transitions in life. Through those messages, I found that every story had this one thing in common: *Plants give us something to look forward to.*

Plants give me, and may others, a reason to want to get up in the mornings. This hobby is a distraction from the chaos of the mind, chaos from the world outside our walls. We become lost in the curves of the leaves, the smells of the soil, and the touch of the stems. It tickles all of our senses. Life comes at us fast. It's inconsistent at times. It's loud. Between appointments, deadlines, notifications, and the weight of the world, we are in a constant state of living among the hustle and bustle. How many times have you been so immersed in to-dos that you realize the day has completely passed you by?

There's a reason why we gravitate toward plants, and it's not just because of their beauty. There is scientific data that proves why we become more grounded and at ease when immersed in nature.

Plants have been shown to:

- Help with stress reduction
- Improve focus
- Ground us to be present in the moment
- Provide nurturing and responsibility
- Improve productivity
- Reduce negative thought patterns
- Lower cortisol (stress hormone) levels
- Promote patience and consistency

The Science Behind the Green Babies

According to a study published by the National Library of Medicine titled, "Interaction with indoor plants may reduce psychological and physiological stress by suppressing autonomic nervous system activity in young adults: a randomized crossover study," twenty-four young male students were broken into two groups of twelve and made to do both computer tasks and plant-related tasks.

This randomized crossover study examined whether actively interacting with indoor plants could reduce stress compared to

go to where it's green

On days when I don't know what to do with the chaos in my brain, I go to the plant nursery. I often say the plant nursery feels like a second home. Walking through those doors feels like stepping into a different rhythm even when I feel stuck. Surrounded by green, I can breathe a little deeper. Being in a space where nothing demands anything from me feels peaceful. I don't have to be productive. I don't have to be "okay." I can just exist among living things that are growing at their own pace. I can wander, touch leaves, and admire new growth. Each visit becomes a gentle form of therapy—the hum of greenhouse fans, the warmth of filtered sunlight, the smell of damp soil. The nursery doesn't fix everything, but it gives me moments of peace, sparks of curiosity, and something living to focus my attention on when I need it. Over time, these small moments add up, helping me find my footing again; one plant, one visit, one deep breath at a time

Plant Pro Tip! Create your own "care corner." Keep your watering can, pruning scissors, leaf cleaner, microfiber cloth, and fertilizer in one spot. A cart with all these items on it can make them more assessable for use around the house and it saves time!

completing a computer-based mental task in young adults. The researchers found that participants experienced both psychological and physiological stress reduction during plant interaction, including lower sympathetic nervous system activity (associated with the body's stress response), reduced diastolic blood pressure, and more positive emotional states such as feeling calm, comfortable, and natural. The findings suggest that hands-on engagement with indoor plants can promote relaxation by suppressing autonomic nervous system activity, supporting the idea that plant care is not just aesthetically pleasing but also beneficial for stress management and overall well-being. (Lee et al. 2015)

This research was no shock to me. We hear it all the time: "Go touch grass!" or "Look deep into nature."

Plants have been shown to support us in ways that often feel subtle, yet grounding. They gently lower stress levels, easing the constant pokes of tension we carry in our bodies, and invite our nervous systems to slow down. In their presence, our minds soften. Focus sharpens with calming and attention. Plants draw us out of the rush of past regrets and future worries and bring us into the present moment, asking only that we notice them as they are.

Caring for plants introduces nurturing and responsibility without pressure. They teach us how to tend to something outside of ourselves, providing us with a sense of purpose and gentle accountability. Through daily plant care rituals, we build routines that anchor us. Productivity often improves, not because we work harder, but because our environments feel steadier, calmer, and more supportive.

Create a Ritual of Care

One of the most healing aspects of plant care is getting into a routine. Those moments of admiring the new leaf unfurling, checking the soil and tilting the watering can to see the water seep out into the saucer below, and checking the undersides of your plants' leaves for pests are giving yourself permission to slow down. Those small tasks are grounding and reconnect us to the present moment. Having houseplants is about creating a connection to nature *outdoors* by having it at the palm of your hand *indoors*.

It's not just about keeping plants alive; it's about creating moments of peace in the process.

Plants also help interrupt negative thought patterns. They remind us that change is natural, that rest is not failure, and that seasons exist for everything. A drooping leaf does not mean we are not good enough; it means something needs to be adjusted. In this way, plants model resilience and adaptability, offering quiet lessons in patience and self-compassion. Growth happens in stages, often slow, and not all progress announces itself right away.

Emotionally, plants provide companionship without expectation. They sit with us during moments of loneliness, transition, and uncertainty. Their presence can soothe anxiety, lift heavy moods, and offer comfort simply by existing alongside us. As houseplant lovers, we've taken it one step further and decided not only to enjoy the beauty of nature outdoors but also to have plants surrounding us indoors by creating a jungle sanctuary that immerses us in plants throughout our day-to-day lives.

Plants also gently reframe how we see ourselves. Through caring for them, our confidence grows. We learn to trust our intuition, to observe before reacting, and to give ourselves permission to learn through trial and error. Over time, we realize that tending to plants is also a practice of tending to ourselves. It allows us to start listening closely, responding with care, welcoming new ideas in our minds, and allowing room for growth and rest.

In loving plants, we are often learning how to love ourselves more patiently and kindly.

Personal Reflection and Connection

Some of my most peaceful moments have been among my plants; early morning watering sessions, quiet evenings pruning leaves, or traveling to see a rare bloom. They remind me that peace isn't always found in grand escapes, but in the simple, consistent acts of care. Every plant I grow carries a story, and each one connects me to the larger cycles of life. Throughout this book, I share some of the stories that have helped me grow, and I hope to encourage you to reflect on your own stories as well, to recognize how far you've come too.

Growing plants can bring us closer to loved ones that are here, but it can also remind us of those who have passed. Maybe you share the love for plants with someone in your family that is no longer with us and being surrounded by plants helps you feel closer to them. During a virtual consultation, I was asked for help with a Christmas cactus (*Schlumbergera* x *buckleyi*) that had been passed down to this woman and her family after her grandmother's passing. This cactus was in the family for ninety years! Now that's an heirloom plant! It was in need

The Thanksgiving cactus (*Schlumbergera truncata*) in bloom. *Schlumbergera* plants are known as "legacy plants" because of their resilience and ease of propagation, making them wonderful plants to pass down for many generations.

of fresh new soil and an increase in light. Once we could improve its health, she also wanted to take cuttings to pass along to other family members to grow in their collections. In turn, that one plant will continue to bring connection to her family for years to come. That's the true beauty of plants.

Being that I create plant videos and provide plant care advice online, I'm accustomed to taking photos of my plants pretty often. This isn't about aesthetics; it is about documenting the newest blooming hoya or the unfurling fenestrated monstera leaf. I also take those pictures and videos and incorporate them into plant care videos at a later time. In the early moments after my husband's loss, I didn't think anything of it since this was normal behavior for me. Some days, I saw no growth. On those days, I grew frustrated because it wasn't happening fast enough. After a month though, looking back at those images, I could see that change indeed was happening.

Plants don't bloom out of pressure; they bloom from their continued care. And somewhere along the way, I realized that I was doing the same. You may not always notice your own growth in real time either. Healing often hides in the background; in the routines you repeat, in the care you give, in the way your heart begins to soften again. One day, without warning, you'll look back and realize you were growing much like your plants all along, although you didn't notice it at the time.

Plant Care vs. Self-Care

You know the airline safety instructions "Put your own oxygen mask on before helping others." I feel this metaphor wholeheartedly. Attending to your own needs first (nutrition, sleep, exercise, and so on) allows you to be able to engage in this hobby of growing plants without feeling completely overwhelmed. If I'm overwhelmed and haven't taken the time to truly care for myself physically, mentally, and emotionally (if I am as dehydrated as the Sahara Desert and I have not eaten to fertilize myself, for example) then I am not "in it to win it" for the plants around me, especially if I have a large collection to care for. Plants and their care are *tools* for me to ease my mind from the chaos, to aid me in my time of need, and to encourage me to slow down. When I have been at my worst and had plants that I hadn't properly cared for, it was a combination that added to my stress, not relieved it. Attend to your own needs first.

If there's one core thing I want you to take away from this book it is that no one should make you feel bad for not sticking with a plant that doesn't bring you joy. If you are not in a space to treat a plant with pests and would rather part ways with it, I welcome it. I want plants to inspire you, to ground you, and to excite you, not frustrate you. I want to teach you the skills to care for your plants at whatever stage you are in, and if that means decreasing the number of plants in your collection to take better care of you, then I'm completely here for it. Remember, your plants can wait, but there is only one of you.

below A slipper orchid (*Paphiopedilum* sp.) is more like us than we think. An orchid blooms because its basic needs are met consistently over time: the right light, the right amount of water, periods of rest, and patience.

opposite Among plants, time slows down and the mind hums quietly.

2

Growing Confidence with Plants

"I don't have a green thumb like them."

You're right, but they didn't have one either. They learned.
They overwatered. They underwatered.
They mixed their soils until they found what works.
They stayed curious and kept practicing.
They faced rot, pests, and heartbreak.
They tried over and over again until thriving became the new normal.

Growth Is Never Perfect

I remember when I purchased my first official plant, Walter the cactus. I felt so much pressure to keep him alive and thriving. I searched for care, lighting, and watering advice. After a solid week, I was a full-blown horticulturist (only in my mind, though). I went and bought ten more plants, including a golden pothos (*Epipremnum aureum)* and a calathea/prayer plant (*Goeppertia zebrina*). Needless to say, that calathea with its

above When light hits a monstera leaf, the shadow it casts isn't smooth or symmetrical. It's full of holes, splits, jagged edges, and unexpected shapes.

opposite An orchid teaches this lesson beautifully. For months it appears stagnant, focusing all of its energy beneath the surface, strengthening roots and leaves with no sign of a bloom in sight. It would be easy to assume nothing is happening, but all that waiting isn't wasted. When the conditions are right and the orchid is ready, it sends up a spike and blooms.

crispy tips was dead in a few weeks. Walter the cactus survived my neglect, but all the others were eaten by thrips in a few short months.

Now if I could turn back time, I may have told myself to slow down, but I'm pretty stubborn and all those dead plants actually pushed me to want to try again. I am naturally very inquisitive, and I like to continue to try something until I know I gave it all I could. What I did differently the next time, though, was take more time to actually watch my plants and to be more aware of their cues, instead of just buying what looked pretty. Once I went into plant care with this mindset, it allowed me to have fun with my plants. I welcomed the opportunity to experiment and was overjoyed when I succeeded. Even now, one of my favorite things to share are plant experiments. From attempting to grow a cactus in water and reviving dying orchid blooms to growing every possible type of exotic fruit from seed on my windowsill, I truly have no idea how the experiment is going to turn out, but that's part of the fun. Different environments will have different outcomes, so seeing it through my own lens and sharing the results on the internet only catapulted my desire to discover more.

Just like our plants, we don't grow overnight. Progress takes time and if you're patient and stick with it, both reward consistency. We could choose to give up completely or we can take those initial challenges and turn them into a desire to succeed even more. Success can come from those failures. Failures often can light a fire under you, making you push through the negatives and the disappointments. When you become so preoccupied with doing things correctly, it takes away from the journey and

the joys of growing. Confidence in any skill doesn't come from being accurate all the time; it comes from experiencing the good and the bad, and making small improvements.
At some point, you'll start making confident choices: repotting when needed, pruning like it's no one's business, and trusting your instincts, instead of spiraling out of control and needing to constantly Google various plant symptoms. Even as you gain these skills, you'll continue to find things that stump you. You'll still lose plants. Everyone does. It won't be as often as before but each one leaves behind a quiet lesson. You'll also watch plants flourish because you figured out exactly what they needed, and that's when you'll understand that confidence isn't about control; it's about connection. By building those skills and trusting your instincts, you'll be amazed with all you can accomplish.

So how do we keep the momentum going and grow our confidence as a new-found plant parent? By following what I call "Leaf Lessons."

Leaf Lesson #1

Learn to Trust Yourself

In a subtle yet very powerful way, plants help build our confidence. Over time, your intuition kicks in and plants stop feeling as scary as they once were. You'll start to have a sense for when your plant needs water. You'll know those spots on your plant's leaves are completely normal. And better yet, the time will come when you find a pest on your plant and it doesn't make you feel like tossing your whole collection into a fire. Every moment spent with your plants is practice in paying attention, trusting your instincts, and learning that mistakes aren't failures, they're feedback.

Some tips on gaining trust with your plants:

- Stick to a small number of plants. Start with a few, grow comfortable with those, and then move on to others if you chose to.
- Instead of asking yourself "What did I do wrong?" change the question to "What could I try differently?"
- Stick to what feels familiar to you when you're first growing. Too much too fast can cause frustration and become overwhelming.
- Propagate a piece of your plant in case growing doesn't go as planned.
- Remember, every dead plant becomes a great teacher!
- Even small progress is a huge reason to celebrate. Look at you grow!

Once I grew more confident in my plant-care skills, I started conducting experiments. I experimented (and still do!) with mixing soils, testing light, and watering in different ways. I'd read science-based educational articles on plants of interest, then practice what I learned and made my own observations. I'd pass along what worked and didn't work with my social media followers and then continue to work with the other plants in my collection. That's when my confidence really began to grow—when I trusted my own rhythm. *From there, the plant rescues happened!* Looking back at it now, I think I instantly gravitated toward plant rescues because it was a reflection of what I felt like internally. Going through the motions of seeing a plant in terrible conditions, then seeing it grow and heal with care, was that external reminder I needed at the time.

A few summers ago, I rescued a peace lily (*Spathiphyllum* sp.) for $3 USD from the

String of hearts (*Ceropegia woodii*) is a trailing plant loved for its tiny heart-shaped leaves. Native to Southern Africa, it naturally grows by creeping along the ground and spilling over rocky ledges, and you'll typically see it growing freely from hanging pots or shelves.

clearance section. I shared this rescue on social media and so many people were rooting for this little plant as I posted an update on it every few weeks. One of the final updates I shared was how this once tiny, wilted, and awful looking peace lily was now green, showing so much new growth, and even had a flower poking its way through. It was the day of my birthday, only two months after my husband's passing, and I was having a very difficult time. My dad held me to wish me a Happy Birthday, and in that moment, he said "You are like your peace lily rescue. When you found it, it looked awful. You went through the process of chopping it, cleaning it up, and awaiting new growth. The more you care for it, the more *you* will grow new leaves, and eventually, you'll get those blooms back, too."

I'll never forget that moment. Thank you Papá for that.

I'm here to say that you'll get there, too. Every wilted leaf, every repotting gone wrong, every pest you battle, they all build experience. And that continued experience—not the hunt for perfection—is what creates confidence.

I know you may hear it as a joke in the online plant community, but sometimes it really isn't you; it was the plant you chose and its inability to thrive in your environment. I'm serious. Take the pressure off yourself, forget about that plant you killed, and try again with another one that brings you joy.

My now-thriving peace lily (*Spathiphyllum* sp.).

Leaf Lesson #2

Start with a Healthy Collection

Starting with a healthy plant collection sets the tone for everything that comes after. I'm never here to discourage you from any plants you have your eye on and there's just so many to choose from, but I would hold off on plant rescues until you gain some confidence. I do thoroughly enjoy the clearance rack at plant shops and nurseries, and although it can be very tempting and I do encourage giving struggling plants a second life, rescue plants can come with a variety of challenging issues—including pests and rot—which can become overwhelming, especially for someone just starting.

When you buy a healthy plant, it comes with these main benefits:

- Stronger plants adapt better to new environments, lighting changes, and routine care
- Fewer pests and diseases reduce the risk of infestations spreading
- Less stress for you and the plant, creating a calmer, more enjoyable experience
- Builds confidence. Success early on encourages consistency and curiosity
- Encourages mindful growth, helping you choose plants that truly fit your lifestyle

In this world of ample opportunities for online shopping, you can have anything sent to your door with the click of a button. The same is true with plants. If you are not careful, that single click of a button will yield a porch full

below This golden pothos (*Epipremnum aureum* 'Neon') is a healthy plant, displaying consistent leaf color, perky leaves, and balanced new growth.

opposite Stressed? Go to the nursery. Sad? Go to the nursery. Having a great day? Celebrate with a new plant at the nursery!

of plants. Believe me, this has happened to me more times than I'd like to admit.

When you're just beginning your collection, buy in-person to know what to look for in future purchases. This is a safe option because you can get your eyes on the plant and do a thorough check on its health.

Check the leaves. Look for vibrant, even color (avoid excessive yellowing, browning, or spotting). Leaves should feel firm, not limp or brittle. Watch for pests and check the undersides of leaves and along the stems.

Inspect the stems. Stems should be sturdy and upright. Avoid plants with mushy, wrinkled, or heavily damaged stems.

Look at the soil. Soil should be slightly moist, not soggy or bone dry. Sniff the soil! Avoid plants sitting in water or with a sour smell (a sign of root issues).

Peek at the roots (if possible). Check the bottom of the plant pot for roots coming out of the drainage holes and look for roots peeking through around the top of the pot. Avoid plants in both situations, as well as plants with roots that are dark or mushy. If you're careful, it is easy to check on plant root health. First squeeze the sides of the pot gently, then pop the plant and the root ball out of the nursery pot, but please be mindful to not damage the plant and avoid creating a mess. Healthy roots are typically white or light-colored and firm.

Notice new growth. Signs of fresh leaves or unfurling growth often indicate an actively growing, healthy plant. Buy from shops or growers that keep plants clean, well-lit, and properly spaced. A well-maintained space usually reflects healthier stock.

Over time, your collection grows not from impulse, but from understanding, setting you up for long-term success, resilience, and a deeper understanding of the plants you bring home.

left When shopping for new plants, slow down and observe. Healthy plants often show their quality quietly.

opposite A close-up of a healthy freshly rooted *Monstera deliciosa* propagating in water. These new roots are smooth, firm, and actively growing, which are clear signs the cutting is successfully transitioning after being cut from the mother plant.

Leaf Lesson #3

Be Patient with the Process and Celebrate All Results

If you're looking for instant gratification—I'm going to hold your hand while I'm saying this—you picked the wrong hobby! Most times, we choose this hobby to slow down; to become more enamored with the beauty around us. We live in a world that rewards instant results, but plants just don't work like that. If you think about it, neither do people. Growth takes time. Plants live on their own timeline and so do we. You may not see the change every day, but the roots are still growing and reaching

down, even though we can't see them. You might hover over a new leaf every morning waiting for the magic to happen and wonder what you did wrong because it is taking so long. You may want to do more to speed up the process or look for products to help it along, but if you are patient enough, the growth will come all on its own.

The beauty of growth is that you don't see it in the day-to-day, but all of a sudden, this little cutting you propagated, has grown its first new root. *You did that!* With your bare hands, you created this new plant that in turn will grow into much more than you imagined.

I learned this lesson from a rubber tree plant (*Ficus elastica*) in my collection. She started off beautifully by growing on my front porch all spring and summer. The weather forecast showed a cold front coming through, so I brought her into the garage for two nights and by the third night, 75 percent of her leaves had dropped. All that growth was now gone. Plus, it was officially time to bring her inside for the cold months, so to encourage more active growth, I set her in front of the sunniest window in my home and made a chop to her stem. After nine months, all her leaves were even bigger and better than before. If I would've given up, I would have missed her in all her beauty.

There are seasons of visible growth and seasons of rest. Both seasons are equally important. The lessons you learn with plants are an extension of your own growth, so stop expecting perfection and start appreciating slow and steady progress.

above The excitement of plants should not stop after buying one. Seeing how it comes to life in your space after all the care you've provided is the best part.

opposite I'm a "feel the leaves" kind of person. Picking the right plant to bring home becomes an art form when taking the time to observe the characteristics of the plant at the plant store.

below Stop holding onto things that provide no value. It's okay to let it go. Losing old leaves is a part of a plant's growth as it makes room for more. Releasing what no longer serves you creates space for new energy, healthier growth, and brighter opportunities.

opposite, top Even in botanical gardens and arboretums where light, humidity, and care are near perfection, you will still find plants with crispy tips. That small imperfection is a reminder that plants are living, adapting organisms, not just decor. Crispy tips don't mean failure; they mean the plant is alive and responding to its environment.

Thriving Beyond Comparison

We are not meant to be "social media perfect." When you spend enough time around plants, you start to notice something beautiful—no two ever grow exactly the same. Even two plants of the same species, sitting side by side and receiving the exact same care, will grow differently.

We scroll through plant pages online and see beautifully curated plant rooms, immaculate greenhouses, perky leaves, and perfect collections. We look at someone else's life and wonder, *Why not me?* Comparison is the thief of joy and plant care isn't a competition or a measure of worth. What we don't see behind those immaculate collections are the droopy leaves, the trimmed crispy edges, the thrips damage beneath the leaves, and all the behind-the-scenes work that makes those moments look effortless. The so-called "imperfections" on plants are often altered or erased to make them more appealing to the masses. We see this everywhere—from dyed orchid blooms to glitter sprinkled on moss and flowers glued onto cacti lining grocery store shelves. These modifications are meant to catch the eye, to make plants look more exciting or polished than they naturally are. Plants don't need embellishment to be beautiful! Their quirks—yes, even the uneven leaves, discoloration, and crispy tips—are part of what makes them alive. Our plants don't need to be embellished and displayed as if they're in a museum; they're supposed to be lived with and loved just as they are.

Every plant, and every person, grows according to their own rhythm. Your orchid

Like a cactus, we are resilient.
Even in the harshest
environments,
we learn to endure.
We persevere.
We find strength in the
waiting.
And when the time is right,
we thrive.
A cactus reminds us
that beauty and growth
can rise from the most
challenging conditions.

may only bloom once a year while your friend's blooms twice a year. Your monstera might take ages to split its leaves while someone else's does it effortlessly. None of that means you're doing it wrong. What it means is that you're nurturing something unique. With that uniqueness comes actual connection. You stop chasing trends—"rare plants," "perfect leaves," "aesthetic shelves"—and start creating spaces that feel true to you. Maybe that's what real confidence looks like—being rooted in authenticity, not approval.

When you nurture yourself like your plants, with patience, curiosity, and gentleness, you realize you never needed to compete to grow. You just needed to be in the right light.

Why paint cactus when they are beautiful as they are? Cacti don't rush their growth, and they don't perform on demand. We have to learn to appreciate their tough, protective, exterior because beneath it is a plant capable of producing some of the most breathtaking blooms you'll ever see, if given time, patience, and the right conditions.

Leaf Lesson #4

Let Go and Lean into the Plant Pot

Sometimes you have to remove old, unhealthy leaves to make room for new growth. Some of your plants may have started off full and lush, and now all you're left with is a plant filled with bare stems. Chop it up! It's scary, I know! I will shriek when chopping every time, but I know it'll work out in the long run. Cutting those stems back can help encourage them to grow back stronger. Propagate what you cut off if you want to keep a piece for insurance! Rooting those propagated pieces can result in a whole new bushy plant in the end. You're missing out on the opportunity to start over because you're holding onto what was, instead of embracing what could be.

If you have plants, they will die. There's no way to sugarcoat it. If someone tells you otherwise, they are the same ones telling you to water your orchids with ice cubes.

I used to gauge my value as a "plant person" on how many plants I didn't kill, and when a plant died in my care, I felt like such a failure. Over time I realized that sometimes, some of those plant casualties were out of my control.

To be a successful plant keeper, you really need to home in on this information:

Although labeled as houseplants, all plants are native to somewhere outside.

We can be good caregivers to these green babies by trying to mimic the conditions of their natural environments. That Monstera you own natively grows up large trees in the tropical rainforest while shooting its aerial roots into the forest floor for support. Those orchids you bought from the grocery store live their best life anchored to trees while getting moisture from the air around them. When you become frustrated that you have crispy tips on your calathea or you're worried that your fiddle leaf fig (*Ficus lyrata*) is dropping its bottom leaves, take a look at where and how these plants grow in nature. A tropical anthurium (*Anthurium andraeanum*) is not going to survive for very long in hot desert sun, and a cactus is going to turn to mush in a tropical rainforest.

To be successful, do all that you can to bring the outside inside. *You* are manipulating *your* environment so these plants feel welcome in your space and thrive! It requires hard work and dedication. Even with all the hard work though, because of many factors, you may not be able to provide a given plant with what it requires to grow. Let's be real; sometimes you forget you have a plant or life is life-ing right now and you are barely able to

confidence care corner

Practice "The Five Senses of Plant Care"

See: Notice leaf color, posture, and new growth.

Touch: Feel the soil moisture and texture.

Smell: Healthy soil smells earthy and damp; sour smells signal trouble.

Hear: Listen for the quiet calm that plant care brings.

Feel: Notice how you feel emotionally before and after tending to them.

The more you engage your senses, the stronger your intuition becomes.

care for yourself at this moment, let alone a plant. This is not about those times (everyone has them). Give yourself permission to let go and know that, although we love plants, it's best to *appreciate* every plant but know that not every species of plants will survive in your home.

Life Is Short. Use Your Free Will and Build Something You Love!

The internet told me not to build a pond in my home, but I did it anyway.

Joy doesn't always come from playing it safe. Sometimes it comes from following curiosity and creating spaces that feel alive and true to you. Not everything needs to be approved or understood by everyone else. Some things are meant to exist simply because they make *you* happy.

When I introduced the idea of an indoor pond on the internet, never did I think it would be so controversial. What felt like a personal and creative experiment to bring more nature into my home suddenly became a debate filled with opinions, warnings, and raised eyebrows:

- "Oh look, a mosquito-brooding chamber."
- "Dumb idea, enjoy the insects, humidity, and water damage."
- "Don't do that! That is so dangerous for your dog."
- "Yeah, a body of water for a wooden house. For sure that won't attract insects and damage the structure."

An indoor water feature brings more than visual beauty into a space. It introduces movement, sound, and a sense of calm that plants alone can't always provide. The gentle flow of water creates a grounding atmosphere, softening a room and encouraging moments of pause in an otherwise busy environment.

But those reactions only reinforced something I already believed: Not everything that brings joy needs universal approval. This pond wasn't built to be perfect or practical for everyone; it was built for me to feel alive, grounded, and true to myself. It was a project to push myself out of the box I sometimes create for myself in fear that something is not going to go as planned. And sometimes, choosing what feels right for your own space is the most revolutionary form of self-care there is.

My indoor pond became more than just a project. It became a reminder that creativity doesn't ask for permission and that living things—plants, water, ecosystems—have a way of grounding us when we let them take up space. Build the thing. Grow the plants. Make the mess. Life is too short to shrink your dreams because someone else couldn't imagine them, and if that person doesn't help pay your bills, pay them no mind.

3

Plants as Companions

How can plants be companions? Sure, they can't talk or give us a hug, but we can still feel their presence and somehow, they can make us feel understood. They listen to us without judgment. (If they could speak, they would absolutely be judging us, though!) They hold space for us in silence. Yes, they can absolutely be demanding and distracting while coexisting with us, but they also create beautiful shadows with their leaves in the light. Compare your space both with plants and without them, and you'll see—the space feels bare and cold when they're not there.

My first plant purchase started off as a way of decorating my space. With time, I wanted to challenge myself to try building a successful new hobby since I failed at this so many times prior. Many years later, there's a calmness that surrounds me when I'm with my plants; when I sit and observe all the new growth in my terrarium, when I count the new leaves, or when I see new vibrant growth unfurling. I get lost in the new roots peeking through the moss, and I can smell the soil. It's a feeling I can't always describe, but anyone who appreciates plants can understand. We worry about their well-being and have a distinct sense of love and compassion for them. We correlate certain plants to experiences in our lives. We look forward to every new growth we witness, and we grieve when a plant so special to us doesn't make it.

There's something so beautiful about the company of those green babies. They're non-judgmental, although sometimes dramatic, and you can be exactly who you are in the presence of plants.

Plants and Their Personalities

If my plants could talk, they'd say I apologize way too often for forgetting to water them as I should. They'd tell you about the time I hacked away at a perfectly lush philodendron with spider mites because I was deep into my seasonal sadness and didn't have the willpower to treat it any other way. They'd say I look ridiculous when I make jungle sounds as I water them in the shower to make them feel as though they're in the rainforest. They'd say I get way too excited to lick on those sweet, nectar-dripping hoya blooms. No doubt they'd tell all my secrets! Although my houseplants luckily can't talk, it doesn't mean they don't have their own quirks and personalities.

One of the things I love most about sharing plant life on social media is showing the joy and unexpected moments that come along with it. Out of all the many plant adventures I've shared, none will ever compare to my attempts at catching my Peruvian apple cactus (*Cereus repandus*) in bloom. I had grown this cactus for four years, and this was the moment I had been waiting for—its very first bloom. Cactus blooms are some of the most impressive flowers anyone will ever witness, but what makes them even more special is that some are night bloomers. Their flowers open only after dark, putting on a brief, dramatic performance before closing by morning, as if nothing ever happened. It's as if the flower is just popping in to say hi to show us its beautiful face and then offer an Irish goodbye as it leaves.

Cereus repandus is primarily pollinated by nocturnal pollinators like moths and bats, perfectly matched to its night-blooming habit. When two buds appeared, I knew the window of seeing the flowers open would be small. Unfortunately, I missed the first bloom entirely, which meant this second one was my last chance. Determined not to miss it again, I set up a time-lapse camera and lights outside to capture what I knew would be a monumental moment. Part of me hoped I might even catch something magical on camera. Maybe a moth or bat stopping by to do its important work. That would've been *epic*! I knew I'd lose my mind watching it!

Just as the bud began showing signs of opening, a massive storm rolled in. I had to make a split-second decision: risk leaving the camera and lights outside in the storm and hope they survived long enough to capture the bloom, or tear everything down and restart the setup indoors knowing I'd likely miss the chance to witness any natural pollination.

Variegated wax plant (*Hoya heuschkeliana* 'Variegata') is known for its white and green variegated leaves with tiny bell-shaped flowers that smell like buttered popcorn.

Within minutes, the storm and its high winds, lightning, and heavy rain was coming my way and here I was outside in my robe, whisking everything indoors just in time to set it all up again and then . . . it happened! The bloom slowly started opening. I stayed up watching the bud slowly unfurl from 9:45 p.m. until nearly 2 a.m., completely mesmerized. By 8 a.m., the flower was already closed, its moment finished as quickly as it began. I luckily was able to capture it all on my time-lapse camera.

That experience was shared and loved by so many on social media, but more than anything, it was a moment I'll never forget. It's a perfect example of how patience, care, and persistence can lead us to something truly beautiful. Some of the most meaningful moments, plant-related or otherwise, are fleeting, and things of beauty are well worth waiting for.

Not all of my plant stories are as poetic, though. I'm currently in a constant battle with my fiddle leaf fig (*Ficus lyrata*), which decided to humble me by dropping all of its bottom leaves after growing beautifully all spring and summer. That fiddle leaf is as dramatic as a

My neon pothos (*Epipremnum aureum* 'Neon') is the encourager. She has survived through my neglect when no other plant made it. She is the plant I take cuttings from when I teach others about propagation. She'll be there when I need her the most.

telenovela star and apparently, it needed to remind me who's really in charge!

Then there is my aloe vera (*Aloe vera*), the resilient queen. She is one of my favorite rescues and she overcame the most amount of rot I've ever seen on a plant. Oh, and also, the calathea . . . she's the silent one because she doesn't live here in my house and is better seen at a botanical garden where they can better offer her what she needs.

When you spend enough time with plants, you'll start to see their personalities shine much like people's do. I've learned to appreciate each one for who they are. We don't all have to be best friends. We don't even have to like each other, but we must know how to respect one another. I can respect that there is value in who they are, even if I don't grow them. Certain plants may not be for me, but they'll make a great companion for someone else in their home, instead of mine . . . except for the majesty palm. No one gets away with having a *Ravenea rivularis* in their home and it living a long life of luxury and growth.

I might also put the fiddle leaf fig in this category. I'm still trying to figure out our relationship. As I mentioned before, this telenovela star acts like she doesn't want to live here, but I somehow put up with her drama of dropping seven leaves when the sunlight doesn't hit her top leaf at a 90-degree angle on a Tuesday afternoon. All this being said, the variety of plants you chose to bring into your home should also be determined by what kind of plant parent vibe fits into your lifestyle. Let's look at some different types of plant parenting so you can decide which one matches your vibe.

I can't help but to appreciate the beauty of a fiddle leaf fig, but I also feel completely betrayed that we just can't get along long enough for her to thrive in my home. Just when I think we're on an upward trajectory together, she drops all her bottom leaves. I think I'll continue to judge . . . I mean admire . . . her from afar.

I purchased this aloe vera for $3 USD in 2022 when I rescued it from a big box store with rotted roots and leaves. Years later, and now rot free, it still continues to grow in my collection. What looked like a lost cause at the time became a lesson in patience and resilience—proof that with the right conditions and a little grace, recovery is possible.

carnivorous challenge

Looking for a carnivorous plant for a little bit of challenge? Add a Venus flytrap (*Dionaea* spp.) to your collection. Two of the coolest facts about them:

- **They can count:** A trap usually needs two to three trigger-hair touches within about twenty seconds to close. This prevents wasting energy closing on debris or raindrops.
- **You may notice their long flower stalk when blooming:** Those long stalks serve a purpose and keep pollinators safe. The elevated flowers are well above the trap leaves so bees and other insects can pollinate without getting caught.

What Kind of Plant Parent Are You?

The Rare Plant Collector

You love the hunt. You know cultivar names, leaf shapes, growth habits, and you probably have a wish list saved of the newest plants coming to market as you anxiously await their arrival. You don't mind extra care steps, specialty substrates, or learning through trial and error. Plants are part passion, part science experiment, and you thrive in that space. You're very detail oriented and research-heavy, so humidity levels, substrate mixes, and light specifications matter deeply. You enjoy learning the *why* behind a plant's needs, not just the basics. Specialized setups like grow cabinets, humidity domes, heat mats, fans, and grow lights are part of your world. Your plants often have better living conditions than most people. You're willing to invest time, money, and effort for the plants that spark joy and challenge you.

The Everyday Plant Parent

The Everyday Plant Parent knows what they like, but they gravitate toward plants that don't demand a full lifestyle change. Your collection is equal parts aesthetic and low drama. You appreciate plants that forgive missed waterings and adapt to your real life. If it needs a humidifier, grow tent, and a whole care routine, it's probably not for you. You thrive on simple routines like weekly/biweekly watering, occasional feeding, and repotting when roots start overtaking the nursery pot. You don't need hard-to-find plants to feel legit. A healthy, thriving "basic" plant is enough to fill your watering can.

above The asparagus fern (*Asparagus densiflorus*) is a dense, fernlike evergreen. Although it has "fern" in its common name, it is not a true fern, but rather it's a member of the asparagus family. It is commonly found at plant nurseries and its delicate appearance hides a surprisingly resilient nature, reminding us that looks can be deceiving when it comes to plant toughness.

opposite *Anthurium radicans* x *luxurians* is a hybrid cross between *Anthurium radicans* and *Anthurium luxurians*. Now found for less than $40 USD, it used to be sold for hundreds of dollars when prices were at their peak.

A sea of hoyas (*Hoya* spp.) started as one small plant grown to maturity. Seeing a plant grow from a small baby to full maturity is one of the most rewarding parts of plant care because you get to witness the entire lifecycle unfold. What begins as a single node or leaf carries all the potential of a full plant.

The Sentimental Plant Parent

For this plant parent, plants hold memories, milestones, and meaning. Each one marks a season of life.

You have grown emotionally attached to plants. You remember who gave each one to you, where you bought it, or what you were going through when it came home. Your plants even have their own names. Caring for them grounds you during transitions, grief, growth, or healing seasons.

It's not about their rarity or the number of plants you have; it's more about their stories and losing one really hurts your heart. A cutting from a friend can mean more than the most expensive plant in the shop. You have a patient and intuitive care style that allows you to tend to your plants gently, noticing subtle changes and responding with care rather than control.

The Aspiring Plant Parent

You're just beginning this plant jungle lifestyle, and you're growing with intention.

At this stage, you choose plants carefully, wanting to get it right and not "mess anything up."

You ask questions, save posts, and grow in confidence with each new leaf. Your collection mirrors your own journey toward patience and self-trust. Right now, you are overthinking everything your plant is doing. Yellowing leaf = the plant is dying! A spot on the foliage = the plant is dying! Overthinking is at its pinnacle, but thankfully, it soon fades with experience.

The Chaotic Keeper

This plant parent thrives in controlled chaos in the best way.

Watering is based on vibes only. Sometimes you're on it and on top of it all. Sometimes it's only when you remember. Somehow, things survive.

You have the epitome of an indoor jungle. Plants everywhere; windowsills, countertops, bathroom corners, "temporary" placements that became permanent. You learn through trial and error. You experiment, observe, adjust, and keep going. You're even surprised at how resilient your collection is. Your plants have adapted to you, not the other way around. Sure, you have occasional plant losses, but in turn, it's created a lot of hard-earned wisdom. Plus, that dead plant just leaves space for another one.

A Swiss cheese plant (*Monstera deliciosa*) is a gateway plant for many plant enthusiasts. Honestly, it's easy to see why. I mean, just look at the size of the leaves! They feel bold, dramatic, and almost unreal, giving you that instant indoor jungle vibe.

Crossover Parenting

Most plant parents don't fit into just one category. You might be an Everyday Plant Parent with one rare plant obsession. Or maybe you're a Sentimental Plant Parent who waters like a Chaotic Keeper.

I started my collection with cactus and succulents. I collected at a much slower pace when I started. But by the time I really dove into tropical houseplants, the houseplant craze was at an all-time high right before the COVID-19 pandemic and it skyrocketed as we were in the thick of it. There were plant sales on Facebook groups, plant sellers online were having auctions, price gouging was happening, and you had to comment "sold" as fast as your fingers could type in hopes of beating someone else who wanted the same plant. There wasn't even a moment to think about your actual desire for this plant; it was more about beating someone else to the purchase.

Plants were getting stolen from shops, nurseries, and even botanical gardens. The hunt for these "rare" plants, specifically Aroids, had the same energy as finding Black Friday deals in the 1990s. It was pure pandemonium. I use quotation marks around the word rare because it was thrown around so much, especially at that time. According to the Unites States Department of Agriculture, "rare" in nature is defined as, "Rare plants may be scarce because the total population of the species may have just a few individuals, or be restricted to a narrow geographic range, or both. Some rare plants occur sparsely over a broad area. Other rare plants have many individuals, but these are crowded into a tiny area; in some cases, a single county or canyon. A third kind of rare plants are those with both few individuals *and* a narrow geographic range: these are the very rarest plants."

Commercially, "rare" plants are plants that have yet to reach the mass market and have not yet been easily available for purchase. This wasn't about being rare because of a plant's extinction risk; a plant was labeled rare because of high demand and slow supply. These plants were being sold for thousands of dollars when they were novelties, not true rarities.

Instead of using the term "rare," I like to refer to them as "harder to find" plants. Prices for these plants went into the hundreds to thousands of dollars. I once spent $30 USD on a Monstera Peru (*Philodendron opacum*) leaf cutting. This plant had a small stem with a node attached, no roots, and one leaf. I ordered in the middle of winter and it was delivered to my home and placed in my mailbox. That cutting spent two hours in the mailbox, and by the time I was able to get to it, the cutting was brown and dead from cold damage. That was my first time experiencing the loss of a harder to find plant purchased online at that high of a price. It was at the beginning of what became the madness of auction purchases by so many plant parents. Mind you, now, many years later, that same plant is worth $19.99 USD for a full 6-inch (15 cm) pot. That's wild! Moral of the story: Don't feel the need to go chasing trends. If you wait long enough, that wish list plant will come down in price significantly.

I have since transitioned from the world of harder-to-find plants and have come back to my basic girls again. Call me a frugal queen, but the days of buying high-priced plants are pretty much over for me. You'll now find me at the plant clearance rack at my local nursery, or on the hunt for unique plants I can teach others about.

So, I guess in this season of my life, I'm an Everyday Plant Parent with a mix of Sentimental. I do love to hold onto plants that tell a story.

If you are in the Aspiring Plant Parent category, I want to make sure I am setting you up for success. Don't be like me when I first started and walk into a store with no prior knowledge of the plants you find there and then fill up your cart with them. In the store, that filled cart will feel so green and serene, but once you have those plants in your home, chances are you will feel overwhelmed. I'm here to make sure you play the long game with plants, and the coming chapter outlines a lot of what you need to know for success.

4

Indoor Plant Care Essentials

What starts as a hobby will quickly turn into a rabbit hole of plant-care items you never knew existed. From pots to trellises, grow lights to propagation containers, you can make this hobby as expensive as you want, but my whole goal here is to make plants and plant care accessible to all. There are various ways you can reuse and recycle items for your plants, like old takeout containers. For plant collectors, jars are like gold for plant propagations! I get it, sometimes that new plant gadget is all the rage and they can be fun, but when growing plants, the core essentials will be what keep your collection thriving.

With so much information available to us in the palm of our hands, finding plant care tips is simple. On the flip side, though, having so much information can feel overwhelming and what in the world does "bright, indirect light" actually mean anyway?! Once I took the time to learn how each one of my houseplants actually grows in nature, their needs made much more sense to me. I took that knowledge and did my best to mimic those conditions indoors. Plants are not Pokémon, and we, in fact, don't have to catch them all. The key to growing a successful and overall stress-free indoor jungle is to find the plants that will thrive in your home's conditions, versus having to change your home for the plants you are inviting in. Growing plants can feel less intimidating when we understand the three core plant needs.

Plants from left to right: *Rhipsalis baccifera*, *Hoya linearis*, and a variegated *Dischidia ruscifolia* hanging in front of my south-facing window. This location receives bright morning light and afternoon light until about 1 p.m.

"What plant can I have growing in a bathroom with no windows?" Me: "A fake one!"

Plants Need Light, Water, and Nutrients

Once we have the basics down, we can start to venture off into potting soils, humidity levels, plant accessories, pots, and so on. But I don't want to lose you there, so don't you fret! Let's start at the beginning with the first of the three essentials—light.

We All Need Light to Thrive

Imagine this: You move into a new home. How exciting! A new setup, new possibilities, and a fresh start! The twist, though, is that you are only allowed to sit in a dark corner of that home. All the light you'll ever receive comes from a window 10 feet (3 m) away. You are yearning for an ounce of warmth from the sun's rays, but that far-away window is all that you're allowed to take in. How happy would you be? I don't know about you, but I'd be pretty miserable. That's exactly how many plants feel when they're placed too far from a light source.

When we think about lighting in our homes, we don't all have the luxury of large windows with golden rays pouring in all day and that's okay. You can still grow plants successfully indoors when you understand how light works and how to work *with* what you have.

Light can come from natural sources, like windows or skylights, or artificial sources, like grow lights. Different plants have different light exposure preferences. One thing is for certain, though—light is nonnegotiable. No matter what soil, fertilizer, or pot you use, no plant will survive without light. Even low-light tolerant plants still need light to survive. Light is energy. It fuels photosynthesis, supports growth, and keeps plants functioning at their most basic level. When you give your plants the light they need, everything else falls into place.

Light Is Food for Your Plants

Photosynthesis is "the process by which green plants and some other organisms use sunlight to synthesize foods from carbon dioxide and water" (Oxford University Press, n.d.). Without light your plant will not survive for very long.

A plant's leaves gather light by using chlorophyll, which is the green pigment in their cells, and converts the energy into food. From there, the chlorophyll transforms carbon dioxide from the water and air in the soil and converts it into sugars to feed themselves. No light equals no food.

My hanging pendant grow light.

measuring light

An essential product you may want to invest in is a light meter. It takes the guesswork out of knowing the output your lights are providing. It can help determine how far to have the plant from the lights. Change the setting to FC (foot candles) and place the meter directly under the leaf closest to the light.

Low-light plants (50 to 250 foot candles of light): Peace lilies, calatheas

Medium-light plants (250 to 500 foot candles of light): Hoyas, peperomias, ferns

High-light plants (500 to 1,000 foot candles of light): Monsteras, fiddle leaf fig, rubber trees

Very-high-light plants (over 1,000 foot candles of light): Cactus, succulents

The light can come from either the sunlight or artificially through the use of grow lights. There are so many to choose from, but what we'll be focusing on in this book are the white LED lights you're accustomed to seeing. They are efficient, fairly inexpensive, and strong enough to grow the majority of the plants we look to grow in our homes. It's also helpful to set your grow lights on timers, making them more efficient and one less thing for you to think about. You can find automatic timers that plug into outlets and require you to physically set the times on a dial, or plug-in timers that can be set via Bluetooth. The standard is to keep those lights on twelve to fourteen hours a day. I keep mine set from 8 a.m. to 8 p.m. daily.

Finding a lamp or hanging pendant light and adding a grow bulb can be a great way to both style your plant space and give your plants the light they need. It allows you to blend function with design, turning plant care into part of your home décor rather than something that feels purely practical. Floor lamps, table lamps, and pendant fixtures can all be repurposed by adding a grow light bulb to support plant growth while adding warmth and intention to a room. Before setting things up, always check the lamp and bulb specifications to make sure they're compatible. Pay attention to wattage limits, socket size, and whether the fixture can handle the heat output of a grow bulb. Some grow bulbs can get extremely hot, especially when they're on for twelve to fourteen hours a day—so be careful. Positioning matters too! Placing the light close enough to the plant ensures it actually receives usable light, not just ambient glow. But having the light too close can fade and burn leaves, so keep the foliage from directly touching the bulb. Using a timer can help create consistency and take the guesswork out of daily light cycles.

If you are sunlighticly-challenged (as I like to call it) in your home, then grow lights will be your best option. I grow the majority of my collection under grow lights, and one of the biggest upsides is control. You get to

My rabbit's foot fern (*Davallia solida* var. *fejeensis*) sits under a grow light bulb tucked into a lamp I found at an estate sale. It's a perfect blend of old character and new growth. This plant's fuzzy rhizomes spill over the pot like little paws, thriving in bright, consistent light while adding softness and texture to the space.

decide *where* plants live and *how long* they receive light each day, instead of being limited to window placement.

I keep my lights on for twelve hours a day, with the majority of them set on Bluetooth-controlled timers from 8 a.m. to 8 p.m. This consistency removes guesswork and helps my plants maintain steady growth year-round, especially during the darker months. Grow lights also allow you to create "plant moments" in spaces that would otherwise be off-limits (hallways, corners, shelves, even entire rooms dedicated to plants).

As for the cons, yes, even though grow lights are LEDs, they can increase your energy bill. Unless you have over twenty-two lights like I do, you may not notice a dramatic difference. The more lights you add, the more raised eyebrows you might get from neighbors wondering *what exactly* you're growing in there. And while I can't promise your house won't be visible from the moon, I *can* promise your plants will be thriving.

What About Growing Using Sunlight?

When someone says "bright, indirect light," it sounds vague and even a little frustrating. What does this actually mean?! How can light be bright but indirect? The phrase is often used to describe a location near a sunny window that receives plenty of natural light without sitting directly in a harsh sunbeam. But even that explanation can feel confusing without context.

First, it's important to understand that an indoor plant is almost never receiving true direct sunlight. The window itself filters and softens the sun's rays as they pass through it. True direct light happens mostly outdoors, when there is nothing between the plant and the sun. No glass, no overhangs, no trees, just uninterrupted sunlight hitting the leaves. Indoors, even "direct" light through a window is significantly less intense than direct sunlight outside.

One of the easiest ways I like to explain bright, indirect light is to think about what your plant can see. Place yourself where the plant sits and look around. How wide is its view of the sky? Is the window partially blocked by trees, neighboring buildings, or an overhang? Are blinds cutting off light before it ever enters the room? Do sheer curtains diffuse the sun's rays and soften the intensity? All of these factors shape the quality of light your plant receives.

South-Facing Windows
(brightest and most consistent)
South-facing windows provide the strongest, longest-lasting light, especially in winter when the sun sits lower.

Great for:
- Fiddle leaf fig
- Monstera
- Ficus
- Cactus
- Succulents
- Tradescantias

East-Facing Windows
(gentle morning light)
East-facing windows provide soft, direct morning light, then lower light in winter.

Great for:
- Pothos
- Philodendron
- Hoyas
- Peperomia
- Orchids

West-Facing Windows
(strong afternoon light)
West-facing windows are best for medium to high-light loving plants that can tolerate heat with intense afternoon sun.

Great for:
- Monstera
- Ficus
- Snake plants
- Succulents
- Cactus

Pull plants back a few feet if leaves start fading or crisping under too much light.

North-Facing Windows
(lowest light)
Lower-light tolerant plants are best here since these windows rarely get direct sun.

Great for:
- African violets
- Marantas
- Thin-leaved ferns
- Peace lilies
- Heart leaf philodendron
- Syngonium
- Scindapsus

**Note: Reverse these cardinal direction exposure levels if you live in the Southern Hemisphere.

While plants like African violets (*Streptocarpus* sect. *Saintpaulia*) can *survive* in lower light conditions, that doesn't always mean they will *thrive* or produce flowers there. Flowering is an energy-intensive process, and even plants that tolerate low light usually need brighter, more consistent light to bloom.

a few plant placement truths

- Distance matters: Light intensity drops quickly just a few feet from a window.
- Seasons change everything. Plants may need to be moved in winter.
- When in doubt, *watch the leaves*: stretching = needs more light; scorched = too much.

Plants are incredibly intelligent and when you really home in on their behavior, it'll answer many of your questions, especially about light. If you're growing plants by a window, pay attention to the leaning and the rocking of your plants. The way a plant is leaning can show you it's in need of more light. The phenomenon of the stem lean is called *phototropism**.

In layman's terms, phototropism is when a plant bends toward a light source to increase the amount they are receiving.

Here's some visual plant signs your plant may be communicating to you:

- Stretching or leaning toward a window = not enough light
- Slow growth = light too weak
- Crispy edges or bleached spots = light too strong

***Phototropism:** the orientation of a plant or other organism in response to light, either toward the source of light (positive phototropism) or away from it (negative phototropism). *Oxford English Dictionary.*

Light also changes constantly throughout the day and across the seasons. Morning light tends to be softer and cooler, while midday sun is stronger and more intense. In summer, the sun sits higher in the sky, often flooding rooms with brighter light for longer periods. In winter, the sun stays lower, allowing light to reach deeper into rooms but for fewer hours overall. This is why a plant that thrives in one spot during summer may suddenly struggle in winter, even though you haven't moved it.

Understanding that light is dynamic, not fixed, helps remove a lot of frustration from plant care. You may need to rotate plants for even growth, pull them back from windows in summer to prevent leaf burn, or move them closer and supplement natural light with grow lights during darker months. None of this means you're doing anything wrong; it simply means the environment has shifted.

When you learn to observe how light moves through your home, you gain a huge advantage. "Bright, indirect light" stops being a confusing phrase and starts becoming something you can see, feel, and adjust to. Light is seasonal, flexible, and always changing. Learning to work with it is one of the most powerful tools to keep your plants healthy year-round.

Watering: Finding the Balance

The terms underwatering and overwatering sound simple enough but, in my opinion, they can be confusing for anyone just starting to grow plants. Also keep in mind that growing houseplants and watering them is so much different than growing plants outdoors.

Overwatering = providing too much water too often (frequency *not duration)*

Underwatering = not providing the adequate amount of water the plant needs

To simplify this, let's use a cactus as an example. We know that a cactus is a desert plant and in nature it lives in extreme conditions (dry air, high heat, drought conditions). In our homes, we try to mimic those conditions as best as we can by providing it with a high level of light whether it be a grow light or the sunniest window in our homes. Now, you may think that since this

Plants, of course, will thrive with only natural light too, as evidenced by my monster of a monstera.

plant is a desert cactus, you only need to give it a few drops of water or you're overwatering it. But, back to nature we go! Yes, cacti can go a long time without water, but what happens in the desert when the wet season comes (most deserts experience a distinct wet season, often either in the form of winter storms or summer monsoons)? That cactus is getting soaked and fully saturated on those monsoon days. Now, back in our home, yes, our conditions are different but, when our cactus soil is dry, if we give just a few drops, it will not be enough to get through the soil and down to the roots to sustain the cactus. What should we do instead when the soil is completely dry? Drown that hoe (also known as *water thoroughly*)!

However, if we were to give that same cactus a little water on Monday, and we were feeling gracious and gave it some more on Wednesday, and then your family came over and gave it a little spritz of water on Friday and Saturday—that soil has stayed damp all week. *That* is overwatering. And it will potentially kill your cactus.

Different plants will need different care methods at different times, so checking your plants soil and watching for certain signs on the plant itself will tell you when to water.

This is where plant care can get tricky, trying to figure out what each different plant needs.

Checking the Soil Before Watering

I'm a terrible baker, so don't ask me for a recipe for cookies, but I do know the trick to see if the dough is baked enough in the middle—a toothpick! If the dough sticks to the toothpick, the cookies still need a little more time in the oven, but if the dough doesn't stick, you are ready to pull those treats out for eating. Turns out that the same goes for checking to see if a plant needs to be watered.

Using a probe

Using a soil probe, like the metal one shown in the photo at right, can help check the soil for moisture levels. Inexpensive tools are just as efficient: wooden skewers, a chopstick, or a bamboo stake. They are perfect for deep pots where fingers can't reach down to feel the root zone. Even a popsicle stick gets the job done—anything long enough to be able to get down into the soil. Here's how it works: Slide your tool into the soil a few inches down into the pot. If soil clings to it when you pull it back out, the roots are still hydrated. Give it more time before you water. If the tool comes out mostly clean and dry, the plant is ready for a drink. It's a simple pause-and-check habit that saves plants from being loved a little too much (overwatered) and teaches you to respond to what's happening below the surface.

Use a metal probe to gauge the moisture in the soil.

Other Cues to Use

Remember when I said plants are great communicators? We just have to learn how to listen. Here are a few additional ways to know when your plant is ready to be watered.

Read the Plant, Not the Calendar

- **Ignore schedules.** Seasons, light, temperature, and growth cycles all change how fast soil dries. A "once a week" rule rarely works long-term.
- **Growth phase matters.** Actively growing plants drink more; resting plants slow way down.

Watch the Leaves

- Subtle drooping can mean thirst (especially in pothos, peace lilies, calatheas, orchids).
- Wrinkled or soft leaves in succulents = dry roots.
- Loss of sheen or slightly dull leaves often appear before full wilting.
- Curling inward can be a quiet early signal.

Check the Soil Color and Texture

- Dry soil is lighter in color; wet soil looks darker and richer.
- Crumbly and dusty usually means dry.
- Cool and slightly compact means moisture is still present.

Use the Pot Itself

- Use the lift test. Watered pots are heavy; dry pots feel surprisingly light.
- Drainage holes tell a story. If plant saucers are still damp, wait.
- Terracotta pots dry faster and show moisture stains. Use that as a visual cue.

Pay Attention to Timing and Environment

- Bright light = faster drying
- Warm rooms and high airflow speeds evaporation.
- Humidity slows soil drying, even if the top looks dry.

Match the Plant Type

- Tropical plants prefer evenly moist (but not soggy) soil.
- Succulents and cacti want soil completely dry before watering again.
- Aroids (monstera, philodendron, and so on) like a partial dry-down between waterings, but not to be bone dry.

Learn your Plant's "Thirst Tell"

- Some plants dramatically faint (peace lilies).
- Others whisper (ZZ plants [*Zamioculcas zamiifolia*], snake plants, and so on).
- Over time, you'll recognize *your* plant's unique signal before stress sets in.

When in Doubt

- Waiting one extra day is almost always safer than watering too soon. It's much easier to help a thirsty plant than to have to rescue and restart one that has been drowning.

A simple spray and wipe is all you need to keep your plants dust free.

those leaves are filthy! don't forget to clean them

Leaf cleaning is not just for show; it's a fundamental part of plant care. The leaves are the solar panels of your plants and when there are dust particles on them, they reduce that plant's ability to soak up the light they need to photosynthesize and grow to their fullest potential.

I'll be honest though, when you have a large houseplant collection, leaf cleaning can feel like cooking a big bowl of rice one grain at a time. Dirty leaves can be a major reason why your plant is not accessing light as it should. Even a simple hose-down of the leaves outside or in the shower can make an impact. Now if you want to get really into it, grab your favorite commercially made foliage cleaner—or you can DIY and make your own (see my favorite recipe at right)—to get that foliage shining for all to see. If there's a homemade option that makes more so I don't have to spend more, I'm going to use it, so I choose to always have my own DIY cleaner on standby.

There are many variations of DIY cleaners that are good to use on plants but here's my recipe with items I always have stocked.

In a 16-ounce (455 ml) spray bottle, mix:

12 ounces (340 ml) distilled water
4 ounces (114 ml) ready-to-use insecticidal soap (not a concentrate)
2 to 3 drops peppermint castile soap (Do not use dish soap. It is too abrasive and can clog the stomata [leaf pores]).
2 tablespoons (35 ml) cold-pressed neem oil

Fertilization is an important part of houseplant care, as long as it's done correctly.

Fertilizing: We All Get Hungry Sometimes

Fertilizing plants is a key component of plant care because it replenishes nutrients that plants naturally use up as they grow. In nature, nutrients are constantly recycled through soil organisms, decaying matter, and rainfall. In our homes and gardens though, that cycle is limited, especially in pots, so fertilizing helps provide the nutrients our plants need.

The two most common types of fertilizer are organic (plant or animal-based materials) and synthetic (human-made). An organic fertilizer's nutrients come from things like compost, worm castings, bone meal, blood meal, kelp, fish emulsion, or manure.

A synthetic fertilizer is a man-made fertilizer created from chemically processed nutrients. These fertilizers are made to give nutrients in a precise, readily available form, which means plants can absorb them almost immediately, whereas organic fertilizers focus on long-term, sustainable growth rather than quick results.

Fertilizers typically contain specific ratios of nitrogen (N), phosphorus (P), and potassium (K) often shown as the N-P-K numbers on the label. In synthetic fertilizers, because the nutrients are already in a plant-useable form, they work fast, making them useful when a plant needs a quick boost or is showing nutrient deficiencies.

NPK! You'll hear this a lot when learning about fertilizers. The way I remember what each letter stands for and its function is to break it down.

N Nitrogen (leaves): helps leaves grow

P Phosphorus (feeds): helps roots, flowers, bulbs, and fruits grow

K Potassium (disease): helps plants resist disease and maintain overall health

The trade-off is that synthetic fertilizers don't improve soil structure or microbial life the way organic fertilizers do. If overused, they can lead to salt buildup, root burn, or reliance on frequent feedings. There's no need to be fearful when adding fertilizer to your care routine, just follow the instructions on the label and it'll show you exactly how much to use per gallon or liter of water. When used correctly and diluted properly, they can be an effective, predictable option, especially for container plants where nutrients are easily washed out.

In short, synthetic fertilizers are about speed and organic fertilizers are about longevity.

Without enough nutrients, plants may survive, but they often grow slowly, produce fewer leaves or flowers, and become more susceptible to stress, pests, and disease. I know when I start to see my plants succumbing to pests, I've either gone too long in between waterings and it's stressed them out or I haven't been consistent with fertilizing. Fertilizing also supports long-term plant health, not just visible growth. Proper nutrients help plants photosynthesize efficiently, recover from pruning or repotting, and gain the energy they need to bloom or fruit. When done correctly—at the right strength and during active growth— fertilizing isn't about forcing growth, but about supporting the plant so it can grow the way it's meant to.

previous Have no luck getting your orchid to bloom? Light, environmental care, and fertilizing are key! Fertilizer is especially important to orchids because they don't grow in nutrient-rich soil like most houseplants. In nature, some orchids are epiphytes, meaning they grow attached to trees or rocks. Their roots are exposed to air and rain and receive nutrients only in tiny, diluted doses from decaying leaves, bird droppings, and mineral-rich water that washes over them. In our homes, orchids rely on fertilizer to replace what they would normally receive in the wild. Fertilize regularly when the orchid is not in bloom, and dilute the fertilizer or stop fertilizing entirely when the orchid is in bloom.

Fertilizer Forms

There are four basic forms of fertilizer to consider.

1. **Water-soluble fertilizer** is the term used for a fertilizer that dissolves in water. Some synthetic brands are dyed blue and most look like small grains. Others are more dustlike. It is mixed into irrigation water and applied when you water your plants. Can be organic or synthetic.

2. **Liquid fertilizer** is already in liquid form and comes in a bottle. Sometimes it is a concentrate that you need to mix with water, and other times it comes already diluted. Read the label to know which one you have. Can be organic or synthetic.

3. **Granular fertilizers** are little pellets that are sprinkled around the base of your plant onto the soil, and they release their nutrients

whenever you water or as soil microbes break them down. Can be organic or synthetic.

4. **Slow-release fertilizers** are tiny, round orbs made of fertilizer encased in a soft coating that breaks down over time. Some brands release nutrients for months. Most are synthetic.

Now that you have this info, here comes the million-dollar question: Which one is the best? I, unfortunately, can't answer that question though. It really comes down to your routine and preference. If you water often and like having more control, a water-soluble or liquid fertilizer may be the better fit. If you prefer a low-maintenance approach, slow-release pellets or an organic granular fertilizer can quietly do the work for you in the background. There's no single right answer, just the one that works best with your lifestyle and keeps your plants consistently fed.

Find one you enjoy and stick to it. Your plants will thank you!

Flowering takes *a lot* of energy for a plant like a cyclamen (*Cyclamen persicum*), especially compared to many common houseplants that seldom flower. Cyclamen grow from a tuber and during their active growing season (fall through winter), the plant pulls heavily from that stored energy to produce its upright flowers and patterned leaves at the same time. Because of this, a balanced fertilizer or a higher phosphorus fertilizer formula is beneficial.

Now That's Just Nasty! Plants and Their Pests

I will be the bearer of bad news if I need to be, so here goes. If you have houseplants, you *will* have pests. I'm so sorry but there's truly no way around it. The goal isn't to never have pests; it's to know how to recognize them early and respond with confidence. Where do these suckers actually come from? They're sneaky little selves can hitch a ride from that bouquet of flowers you brought home, fly through the screen of those open windows, or even arrive on your produce from the grocery store! Now that's just plain nasty! Our plants create indoor ecosystems where they interact with microorganisms like fungi, microbes, and unfortunately, pests.

Pests are opportunists who often show up when conditions are just right. They thrive in warm temperatures and humid air, often targeting stressed plants or tightly packed foliage.

The key is understanding that pests are part of the plant experience, not a personal failure. Regular check-ins, and acts like cleaning leaves, quarantining new plants, and learning the signs of common pests, can turn what feels like panic into prevention. When you shift your mindset from fear to awareness, pest management becomes just another part of plant care. It'll eventually become one you're fully capable of handling.

Let me introduce you to some of the most common plant pests and ways you can prevent and manage them.

Fungus gnats

Although they are mostly just a nuisance, fungus gnats can cause damage to your plant through their larvae feeding on plant roots if there's a severe infestation, but they

These tiny, delicate flies thrive in moist conditions in your soil. What makes them even more annoying to plant owners is that they fly and love to inconvenience you in the worst ways possible—like flying straight up into your nose, landing in your morning tea, and wafting you in the face as you sleep!

my favorite method of handling fungus gnats—carnivorous plants!

Yay, a reason to buy more plants! Carnivorous plants like butterworts (*Pinguicula* spp.) and sundews (*Drosera* spp.) help fight fungus gnat problems that often come along with other houseplants. These plants use their sticky leaves to trap small flying insects, slowly digesting them as a nutrient source. This is a natural form of fungus gnat control. Not only are they super cool to watch in action, but they also add a functional layer to your plant collection, working quietly in the background as your little warriors while you enjoy their unique shapes and textures.

are easier to treat and to manage by making some changes in your plant care routine. Fungus gnats love damp conditions. Having soil that stays too wet, not incorporating additional amendments to the soil, or watering houseplants too often can be reasons for an increase in fungus gnats.

Treatment for adults:

- **Sticky traps:** Yellow sticky traps and blue light plug-ins attract and trap the flying adult gnats.

Treatment for eggs/larvae/pupae:
If you have adults, you also have eggs, larvae, and pupae in the soil.

- ***Bacillus thuringiensis* subsp. *israelensis* (Bti):** Bti comes in different forms, like as bits, dunks, granules, or drops. Use as directed on the label.
- **Cold-pressed neem oil:** Use 1 to 2 teaspoons (6 to 12 ml) in a quart (1 L) of water and drench the soil when it's time to water your plant.
- If the infestation is major, remove all the existing soil and replace it with new.

Due to their life cycle, continued treatment is necessary as it can take 5-plus weeks for control. Use any of these treatments weekly until the fungus gnats are gone.

Mealybugs

Small, white, soft-bodied, cottonlike, fluffy, soul-sucking . . . I mean plant-sucking . . . pests. The females, which you'll find most commonly on houseplants, are wingless, but don't let that fool you. They have these stubby little legs that allow them to move efficiently into every crevice of the plant. You'll often spot them along stems, tucked into leaf joints, or hiding at the base of new growth.

What makes mealybugs difficult to get rid of is that they embed themselves into the hard-to-reach areas of a plant, like deep into the stem nodes and leaf folds. They often make their way into new leaves before they even unfurl, causing distortion, stunted growth, yellowing, and overall plant stress before you even realize what's happening. As they feed, they suck sap from the plant and secrete a sticky substance called "honeydew," which can attract ants and lead to the appearance of a black mold on the foliage.

Treatment:

- Prune any severely infested foliage and dispose of those trimmings (I know it hurts to throw them away, but it keeps the pests from spreading to other plants).
- Use insecticidal soap or 70 percent isopropyl alcohol.
  - » Test isopropyl alcohol on a small area first by using a small brush or soft cloth to dab it directly onto visible mealybugs and waiting a few days to see if it negatively affects the plant in any way. If there is no harm to the plant, you can dab all the mealybugs you see.
  - » Remove the plant from its light source until the application is dry. Insecticidal soap and isopropyl alcohol can burn foliage in strong light until the leaves are dry.
  - » Repeat the alcohol treatments every few days, focusing on stems, leaf joints, and new growth where mealybugs like to hide.
  - » Rinse the plant thoroughly after treatment, if possible, to remove the alcohol residue and remaining pests.
  - » Isolate the affected plant to prevent the spread to nearby plants and monitor closely for several weeks.

Root mealybugs are even trickier because they live below the soil surface, feeding directly on the plant's roots. They look similar to regular mealybugs but are often discovered only when a plant is declining for "no apparent reason." Common signs include slowed growth, yellowing leaves, sudden wilting despite proper watering, and a white, cottony residue along the roots or inside the pot near drainage holes.

Because they're hidden in the soil, root mealies can go unnoticed for long periods. When you unpot an affected plant, you may see clusters of white fluff around the roots or notice the soil itself looks dusty or moldy. These pests weaken the plant from the inside out, making these pests especially damaging if left untreated.

Treatment:

- Remove the plant from its pot. Gently rinse all the soil from the roots and inspect thoroughly.

- Soak the entire plant (leaves, stems, roots) in a half-strength diluted insecticidal soap for thirty minutes (for severe infestations, soak for as much as an hour), then repot in fresh soil and a clean pot.
- Isolate the plant during treatment and monitor closely for several weeks, repeating treatments as needed.

Spider mites

To the naked eye, spider mites look like tiny specks scattered across leaves. They are often mistaken for dust. But under a magnifying lens . . . nope. Unfortunately, they are exactly what you'd imagine—tiny spiderlike critters. One of the first visible signs is fine webbing, especially along leaf edges, between stems, and on the undersides of leaves. You may also notice stippling or speckled discoloration on the foliage, where mites have been piercing plant cells and sucking them dry.

Spider mites thrive in warm, dry environments, which is why they're especially common during winter when indoor heating is running or in hot summer conditions with low humidity. Left untreated, infestations can spread quickly and cause leaves to yellow, dry out, curl, and eventually drop.

Treatment:

- Use a strong blast of water to rinse the foliage, paying close attention to the undersides of leaves where spider mites like to hide. This helps physically remove adults and eggs.
- Horticultural oil is effective at smothering the adults and their eggs. Add it to a spray bottle according to label instructions and thoroughly coat all leaf surfaces, stems, and crevices.
- Use 70 percent isopropyl alcohol on a cloth or cotton pad to wipe down leaves. Always test a small area first to ensure the plant tolerates it.
- Remove the plant from the light source until any products used are dry. Oil and isopropyl alcohol can burn foliage in bright light until they dry.
- Repeat treatments every five to seven days until the infestation is under control.
- Increase humidity around the plant, as spider mites dislike moist environments.

Spider mites are persistent but manageable. With consistent treatment, good airflow, and regular leaf inspections, you can break their life cycle and help your plants recover fully.

Thrips

Thrips are small and slender soft-bodied insects ranging in color from yellow, black, or white. These little pests are approximately 1 to 2 mm long with wings so, unfortunately for us and our plants, they do fly at the adult stage. They reproduce very quickly and chances are when you see one, you have many more hiding in the crevices of your plants, especially attacking the new leaves. Damage to the plant usually results in a streaky/stippling discoloration of the tops and undersides of leaves, yellowing leaves, smaller growth, and in extreme cases, plant death.

They cause damage to a plant by taking their beady little mouths and chewing on the foliage and then slurping up the sap, feeding on the plant's tissues.

To reproduce, thrips burrow into the plant's tissue, lay eggs, and as the eggs hatch, they make their way out onto the surface of the leaves. The thrips' life cycle is generally thirty to forty days from egg to adult, which unfortunately means treating is not a one-time shot. A successful treatment will need to reoccur weekly until these pests are gone.

I use a lint roller to capture thrips on my plants' foliage.

Treatment:

- Physical removal of thrips with masking tape, a lint roller, or a forceful spray of water can help remove adults from foliage and stems. This helps reduce their population but will not eliminate the eggs.
- Prune heavily infested and damaged leaves. Physical removal will only kill the larvae and adults, but pruning helps limit spread by also removing the eggs and gives the plant a better chance to recover.
- Thrips thrive in dry conditions. Keeping plants well-watered and increasing humidity can help make the environment less enjoyable for them.
- Use an insecticidal soap. Apply once a week, making sure to thoroughly coat the tops and undersides of leaves where thrips hide. Consistency is key. Remove the plant from its light source until the solution is dry. Insecticidal soap can burn foliage until it dries.
- If infestations persist despite these methods, a systemic insecticide may be necessary. Use one only as a last resort and follow label instructions carefully. Avoid using systemics on plants that will be grown outdoors or around pollinators.

Soil: Building a Healthy Foundation

If you follow along with my videos on social media, you may hear me use the term "chunky soil mix," often paired with a dramatic body-and-arm thrusting dance. It's a playful reminder, but the message behind it is serious—incorporating amendments into your soil to create a chunky mix can make or break your plant's health. Plant health starts at the roots, and if those roots are suffocating due to a lack of oxygen in the soil, you'll keep right on thinking you don't have a "green thumb."

First, let's talk about *why* a chunky soil mix matters.

Unless you're dealing with true bog plants, nearly all houseplants require proper drainage. And no, that pot with a layer of rocks at the bottom and no drainage hole is *not* proper drainage. In order for roots to grow long, strong, and resilient, your soil needs built-in air pockets. These pockets allow excess water to drain away and oxygen to reach the roots. Without airflow, soil stays wet for too long, roots suffocate, and rot sets in. Finding pots with drainage holes is essential for a beginner plant parent, but also pairing those pots with a chunky, well-aerated soil mix takes things a step further. Ingredients like bark, perlite, pumice, Leca, and so on can help break up dense soil, improving drainage while preventing compaction over time.

The result? Happier roots, faster drying cycles, fewer pest issues, and plants that are far more forgiving when your watering isn't perfect.

You may notice that indoor soil mixes don't actually contain any true soil, which is too heavy for indoor growing and may contain pathogens. Instead, they are a combination of other ingredients. Let's take a look at some of the most common components of indoor potting mixes, particularly a chunky soil mix.

Houseplant soil (potting mix) is a specially formulated growing medium designed for plants living in containers, not the ground or the garden. If you've ever compared it to garden soil, I'm sure you noticed that houseplant soil is made to be lightweight, well-draining, and breathable, which is essential because roots in pots don't have access to the same airflow, microorganisms, or drainage they would outdoors.

When roots are healthy, they efficiently take up moisture and nutrients from the soil and deliver them throughout the plant. When you prioritize proper soil, drainage, airflow, and watering, you're not just caring for roots, you're setting your entire plant up for long-term success. Healthy roots are typically white, cream, or light tan. Roots should feel firm and springy, not mushy.

Coco chips (also called "coconut husk chips") are chunky pieces made from the outer husk of coconuts. In plant care, they're used as a durable, moisture-retentive growing medium or soil amendment, especially for plants that like excellent airflow around their roots.

above Soil is a living system that creates balance between water retention and drainage. For plants, the right soil is like the right surroundings for us: not too tight, not too loose, full of nutrients, and with plenty of room to breathe.

opposite A chunky soil mix isn't about making plant care complicated; it's about setting your plants up for success from the start. When roots can breathe, plants can thrive.

Pros:

- Improves aeration, which creates air pockets that help prevent root rot
- Retains moisture without staying soggy; holds water on the surface but drains well
- Slow to break down so it lasts longer than bark or peat
- Improves soil structure without compacting
- Has a neutral pH/slightly acidic pH making it great for epiphytic plants (orchids, ferns, bromeliads, and so on)

Cons:

- Contains no nutrients, so fertilizing is required
- Can hold salts if not rinsed properly, causing harm to plants; poor-quality chips may contain sodium
- Can dry out quickly in very airy mixes or warm environments
- Too chunky for some plants; it may not be ideal for fine-rooted or moisture-loving plants unless blended well with other ingredients

Perlite is made from natural volcanic glass. When this volcanic glass is heated to extremely high temperatures, the water trapped inside rapidly expands, causing the material to pop much like popcorn. This expansion creates the lightweight, white, porous granules we recognize as perlite.

Pros:

- Improves drainage and aeration without adding weight
- Can be used for all houseplants
- Can be used as a propagation medium
- Allows roots to access oxygen

Cons:

- Contains no nutrients
- Very lightweight and floats to the soil surface
- Can create uneven moisture distribution if overused
- Dust is irritating to lungs (always use a dust mask when working with perlite)

Orchid bark is made from natural tree bark (pine bark, hardwood bark, fir bark). The bark is stripped, cleaned, and cut into chunks of varying sizes, then often heat-treated to reduce pests and pathogens before packaging.

Pros:

- Improves airflow, creates large air pockets, slows soil compaction
- Can be used for all houseplants
- Mimics how many tropical plants grow in nature

Cons:

- Breaks down over time, which can compact soil and reduce airflow
- Can dry out too quickly in low-humidity homes
- May initially repel water if it dries completely
- Lower nutrient content

LECA stands for lightweight expanded clay aggregate. It's a popular soilless growing medium used in semi-hydroponic plant care and is especially loved for its clean look and ability to provide excellent airflow around roots. It can also be incorporated into soil mixes and used as a propagation medium.

Pros:

- Excellent aeration for roots
- Reduces risk of root rot
- Reusable and long-lasting
- Clean, pest-resistant, and visually minimalist looking
- Encourages strong root growth when plants adapt well to it

Cons:

- Contains no nutrients, so fertilizing is mandatory
- Some roots may die off before adapting to it
- Needs regular flushing of salt and mineral buildup to avoid root burn
- Initial setup is time-consuming (rinsing and soaking is required prior to use)
- Less forgiving if you miss any care steps

Sphagnum moss is a moss collected from bogs and then dried after harvesting. It is known for its incredible ability to absorb and hold water.

Pros:

- Made from dried sphagnum moss
- Provides moisture retention and soil airflow
- Best for propagation, orchids and other epiphytic plants, moss poles, and terrariums and other enclosures
- Naturally antimicrobial

Cons:

- Not all harvesting is regulated or sustainable
- Can stay wet too long and cause rot if packed tightly
- Breaks down faster than bark
- Encourages mold growth in stagnant conditions
- Not ideal as a long-term solo soil substrate

As you continue with your plant journey, you'll discover the soil recipe that makes the most sense for *you*; one that reflects your environment, your watering habits, and your budget. You may notice your soil drying out too quickly, which could mean dialing back on the orchid bark or chunky additives. Or maybe your soil is staying wet for too long, signaling that it needs more aeration through the addition of more chunky materials. These small adjustments are how you fine-tune your plant care and build confidence over time. Soil mixes are not one-size-fits-all, and that's the beauty of them. Your light, humidity, environment, pot choice, and even how often you forget to water all play a role. Just like my cooking, feel free to measure amendments by what your heart tells you (and maybe your hands and eyes, too). Trust the process, observe how your plants respond, and don't be afraid to tweak as you go.

my favorite DIY chunky soil mixes

Tropical Houseplant Recipe

35% indoor potting soil of your choice
35% coco chips
15% perlite
15% orchid bark

***If I'm not using coco chips then it's:*

50% indoor potting soil
25% perlite
25% orchid bark

Easy Cactus/Succulents Recipe

50% cactus-specific potting soil
50% bonsai gravel or small pumice stone

A One, a Two, and a Three: Repotting Made Easy

Often intimidating for a new plant parent, repotting can feel like a daunting task. When I teach repotting, I tend to show the process in the most aggressive manner possible—all on social media. You'll see me dropping elbows on the pot when removing it and *shimmying that soil to settle it,* which means I am vigorously shaking the new soil into the plant pot to make sure the new soil is settling all throughout the nooks and crannies. The goal is to show that repotting doesn't need to be precious or scary. Plants are more resilient than we think, and a little rough love won't end their life. In fact, repotting is often the beginning of a new, healthier chapter.

Repotting simply means transferring a plant from one pot to another while replacing or refreshing the soil. It's a chance to reset the root environment, improve drainage, and give the plant room to grow. While not every plant needs frequent repotting, knowing *when* and *why* to do it can make all the difference.

Reasons to repot a plant:

- **To refresh the soil:** Overtime, nutrients in the soil wash away and become depleted. Replacing the soil introduces a fresh, nutrient-rich mix that supports healthy growth.
- **Roots are running away or bursting at the seams:** Roots growing out of drainage holes, pushing the plant up and out of the pot, or pushing against the sides of the pot can't take up water or nutrients efficiently.
- **To improve current soil composition:** Plants are often sold in soil that works for a greenhouse or retail environment but not necessarily for your home. Repotting allows you to tailor the mix to your light, humidity, and watering habits.

Repotting gives your plant's roots better airflow, fresh nutrients, and room for healthy root growth. I like doing it at the table so I can take my time and really observe what the plant needs. These small care moments add up to stronger, happier plants over time.

to repot or not repot as soon as you bring plants home

Whether to repot new plants tends to be a very controversial topic in the plant world. This is how I look at it. This newly purchased plant went through so much to get to its new home. Prior to the purchase, it started its life growing at a greenhouse, then it was shipped in a box and in a truck where the temperatures drastically changed, then it was set up at a local greenhouse or shop for who knows how long, before finally arriving at its end destination. That plant is going to need some time to recover before getting poked and prodded yet again. So, the short answer is, no, I don't recommend repotting a new plant as soon as you bring it home. Unless the plant is a rescue that is showing signs of concern, I leave it to adjust to my home and its new environment for a few weeks before even thinking of repotting.

Stepping into the plant nursery feels like walking into a lush, living gallery of greenery and blooms. Prior to these plants being at the nursery, they had a long route of travel to finally get here and be ready for your home.

- **If the plant is showing signs of concern:** Yellowing leaves, stunted growth, or constant wilting can be signs of root issues. This is especially true for plants from clearance or rescue sections. Checking the roots can reveal rot, compaction, or dehydration. The roots often tell the story of what the plant has been through.
- **Plant leaning or becoming top-heavy:** A larger pot can stabilize the plant and allow roots to anchor more securely.
- **Funky-smelling soil:** Smelly soil often points to root rot and is a clear sign it's time for fresh soil.
- **Soil staying wet too long:** If the soil never seems to dry, it may be compacted or broken down, limiting airflow to the roots, and increasing the risk of rot.
- **To reset after pests or disease:** Repotting into fresh soil and a clean pot can help remove lingering issues and give the plant a fresh start.

Repotting is less about following strict rules and more about responding to what your plant is telling you. When something feels "off," checking the roots often gives you the clearest answers.

Choosing the Right Pot and Size

Having so many pots of different sizes, making a decision about which one to use can feel like a tough one. If you're anything like me you have *way* too many pots in your garage but none of those pots seem to be the right fit. So we just keep 1,486 pots just in case we need them. Different pots have different functions. Let's talk more about each type to help make the choice easier for you.

Terracotta pots: Made from clay, terracotta is a porous material with tiny, tiny holes that allow air and moisture to move through. If you are someone who keeps a watering can attached to your hand and loves to water your plants often, terracotta is helpful to pull extra moisture from the soil and dry out plants faster. If you are someone who forgets to water your plants or has a plant that likes to stay more on the damp side (begonias [*Begonia* spp.], peace lilies, calatheas, and so on) this may not be the pot for you. Terracotta make great pots for desert plants like cactus and succulents and their weight when wet can help support the weight of heavier plants.

Ceramic pots: These are made from clay that is then coated with a glossy glaze for a smooth, non-porous surface. Ceramic pots come in many shapes and decorative colors, making them a beautiful display vessel for plants. With the glossy glaze, it holds moisture longer than terracotta. If you have a top-heavy plant, ceramic can be a good companion since the pot itself is heavy enough to support the plant. On the flip side, because of the weight, hauling a ceramic pot around can be quite the task, especially when it's filled with a plant and soil. Ceramic pots maintain moisture unevenly, so check all around the soil to make sure the plant does indeed need to be watered.

Plastic pots: You'll find plastic pots commonly used. When you buy houseplants, more than likely the plants are in plastic pots. They are lightweight, more affordable and durable,

retain moisture well, and come in various shapes, sizes, and colors. Clear plastic pots have become all the rage over the last couple of years. Not only does it allow you to see the roots growing, making it easier to know if it's time to increase the pot size, but it allows you to see if the soil is wet or dry. Having a window to what's going on down below makes plant care that much easier. The cons to using plastic pots, though, is that they are not biodegradable and improper disposal contributes to plastic pollution. Since plastic is non-porous, root rot is more common, so having proper drainage holes is important. By looking at my plant collection, you may think that I plant my plants directly in the ceramic pots or the terracotta, but actually, the majority of my collection is planted into plastic pots and I then use the decorative pots as a cover. It allows me to change up the styling of the plant with ease.

Once you've found what material works for you, it's time to determine what size pot you need.

We Want Our Plants to Live in an Apartment, Not in a Mansion!

Indoors, we unfortunately lack the airflow and light that a plant outdoors receives, so when we use a pot that is too large, that excess soil holds moisture for too long. After a few weeks or months, you may find your plant showing signs of distress. Things to watch for would include:

- Leaf drop
- Leaf browning and yellowing
- Wilting
- Stunted growth
- A sour smell to the soil

Now I may be dramatic, but I will always be honest and this is me, your houseplant tía, telling you to step away from that large pot and check the root ball before determining the right-sized pot.

The general rule of thumb is, after you've exposed the root ball, find a pot 1 to 2 inches (3 to 5 cm) larger than the diameter of that root ball. If your root ball measures about 6 inches (15 cm) across, you want a pot that's roughly 7 or 8 inches (18 or 20 cm) wide. Don't be afraid to whip out a measuring tape for this part. Accuracy here can make a huge difference in your plant's long-term health. With practice,

Contrary to popular belief, giving your plant more room to grow in a very large pot (overpotting) may actually be the reason why your plant has gone to the planty heavens.

Check the root ball. It will tell you how large of a pot you need.

you'll start to develop an eye for it and eventually be able to gauge the best pot size just by looking at the plant.

Depth matters just as much as width. A pot that's too deep can create the same problems as one that's too wide. Excess soil holds onto moisture longer than the roots can use it. This often leads to soggy soil, poor airflow, and an increased risk of root rot. If you're using a deeper decorative pot, don't feel pressured to fill it all the way to the top. It's perfectly fine to add soil only high enough to support the root ball, keeping the roots snug and properly supported.

Once you've selected your potting mix and chosen the correct size and style of pot, it's time to gently plop your plant from its current setup . . . or take an elbow to it to remove it from its current container. As you remove the plant from its pot, pay attention to what the roots and soil are telling you.

If your plant is showing no signs of concern, shaking off some of the extra soil is all that you'll need to do before repotting. Don't feel like you have to break up the root ball. You can even massage the bottom of the root ball to loosen some of that soil off if you'd like.

Inspect the roots and check to see if there's any sign of rot. You can look at the roots, but you know what you can use to easily find out if your plant has rot? Your nose! If you didn't smell the soil, did you even truly check it? (You're judging me, I can feel it . . .) The root ball will smell sour and musty, almost like a swamp, if the roots are rotten. If you're thinking, "That's a no for me, dude," then visually, you're looking to see if the roots are dark and/or mushy. A slight pull of the roots will have them falling right off if there's rot.

Assuming everything looks good, grab your pot and think of this step like building a lasagna—simple layers, no rushing. First, make sure your pot has drainage holes. Proper drainage allows excess water to escape and helps protect your plant's roots from sitting in soggy soil. I like to place a piece of window screen or mesh over the drainage holes first so the soil stays put while still allowing water to flow freely. Then, add a layer of potting soil mix. You're essentially creating layers, like making a lasagna (bottom soil layer, root ball, then more soil to the top). You only need a light layer of soil at the bottom, just enough to elevate the root ball so it sits at the correct height. Then, plop that root ball into the pot on top of the soil, and fill the remaining spaces in the pot with more potting soil. Don't forget this crucial step: *Shimmy that soil to settle it.*

A little shimmying of the soil is not only fun, but it also gives the plant a little shake to settle the soil naturally around the roots. This helps eliminate hidden air pockets that can cause uneven watering or root stress. Add a bit more soil if needed but avoid packing it down tightly. Roots need airflow just as much as they need support.

Once everything is in place, water the plant thoroughly until you see water flowing out of the drainage holes. This helps the soil settle even more and ensures the roots are fully hydrated after the move.

Finally, place your freshly repotted plant in a well-lit spot or under a grow light and give it time to adjust. Some plants may pause growth briefly after repotting, and that's completely normal. You've done the hard part. You've successfully repotted your plant! Great job, friend!

Smell the root ball during transplant. A sour or musty smell could indicate root rot.

Make Plant Care a Part of Your Routine

It's much more manageable to balance plant chores when you have a smaller collection, but when your houseplant collection starts to get into the double and triple digits, navigating care tasks can feel harder to balance. What once felt calming can quickly turn into a checklist of tasks if you don't create a rhythm that works for you.

With 300+ houseplants in my collection, I had to shift how I care for them all and intentionally weave plant care into my daily and weekly routines, making it something I look forward to rather than something I avoid. At its core, having plants in the home is supposed to bring a sense of peace. Plant care is as much for you as it is for them. When approached with intention, it becomes a grounding ritual instead of a chore.

- Pick one "Plant Day" each week to do a full check of soil health, pruning, and watering if needed.
- Spend fifteen minutes a day with your plants.
- Pair your plant care time with tea, music, or journaling for a mindful moment.
- Take a few minutes to notice new growth. Tiny new leaves are reminders that your care is working.

One additional tip that has made care easier is to keep plants in high traffic areas. This has helped me to keep track of their needs because I suffer from a case of "If it's not visible, it doesn't exist" syndrome. In addition, grouping plants with similar care needs together and using simple reminders or routines has also helped reduce the mental load of tending to my plants.

opposite Keeping my thirstier plants hanging in a common area of my home is one way I make sure I don't forget to keep them watered. When plants are placed where I naturally pass by them each day, they stay top of mind. I'm far more likely to notice subtle changes like slightly drooping leaves or dry soil, and respond before it becomes a bigger issue.

previous Ready, set, repot!

they're out there lying to you! houseplant myths

Part of houseplant care is the fun that comes along with it. Experimentation is fun, and I always encourage it. Trying new things, observing how plants respond, and learning through experience is how confidence grows over time. That curiosity is what makes plant care feel less intimidating and more personal.

With that being said, not every tip floating around in the world is rooted in plant science. Some advice gets passed down, shared online, or goes viral simply because it sounds clever or convenient. And some of it is just plain wild. I'm talking directly about the suggestion of using mayonnaise as a leaf

shine. Let's leave the mayo in the fridge or on your sandwich, please!

Let's break down common houseplant myths, explain why they don't work, and replace them with simple, practical truths so you can experiment with confidence.

Myth #1: Misting increases humidity
Misting only makes leaves wet for about five minutes and then that moisture quickly dissipates into the air. The water vapor evaporates so fast that it does not meaningfully raise humidity levels around the plant. Same goes for pebble trays under plants. Pebble trays may add moisture to the air, but not enough to change the environment in a meaningful way, unless they're in an enclosed environment like a grow cabinet. Humidity is about the amount of moisture in the air over time, not brief surface moisture on leaves. Actually, frequent misting can sometimes do more harm than good. Wet leaves without proper airflow can encourage fungal issues, leaf spotting, and bacterial problems, especially if a plant is sitting in cooler temps or lower light conditions. At the end of the day, if the act of spritzing leaves is part of your relaxation routine with your plants, who am I to tell you what to do? But if you are looking for ways to actually increase humidity, group plants together, use a humidifier, place a plant under a humidity dome, or grow your plants in cabinets or terrariums.

Myth #2: Bigger pots mean faster growth
Too much soil = too much moisture. Large pots contain more soil than the plant's root system can use. The bottom soil stays soggy while the root ball sits in damp conditions for days or even weeks, leaving you with a soupy bacteria and fungi soil concoction that promotes rot. Plants grow best when their roots are comfortably snug, not swimming.

I don't jump out of plants to *scare* you. I jump out of plants to *save* you from weird plant advice. Every plant you take, every repot you make, every pot you shake, I'll be watching you . . .

Myth #3: Use coffee grounds, banana peels, and eggshells as a fertilizer

These kitchen scraps are not fertilizers in their raw form and adding them directly to houseplant soil can do more harm than good.

Coffee grounds don't instantly "add nitrogen." Fresh grounds can compact soil, hold too much moisture, and encourage mold. Used grounds still need to fully decompose to be beneficial. Banana peels don't release potassium to plants right away. In pots, they rot, smell, attract pests, and can create fungal issues. Eggshells won't provide usable calcium unless they're finely processed and broken down over time, which doesn't happen effectively in containers.

Plants absorb nutrients in specific, soluble forms. This is why you'll see the NPK numbers on properly formulated fertilizers, whether organic or synthetic. These are far more reliable and predictable for houseplants. A balanced fertilizer, used at the right strength, delivers nutrients directly to the roots in a way plants can actually use.

Kitchen scraps belong in compost, where they can fully decompose and transform into something beneficial. Once composted, they become a much safer and more effective way to support plant growth. Actually, while we're at it, let's just keep all food items away from houseplants in general.

Myth #4: Use ice cubes to water orchids

"But Grandma used to water this way, and it worked for her." Look, truly no shade to Grandma and many orchids *survive* this method, but surviving isn't the same as thriving. When we think it through, how much water does an ice cube actually hold? Definitely not enough to fully saturate the orchid's substrate. Most of the moisture only reaches the top layer, leaving the roots below dry.

You'll even see some care tags that say "Use three ice cubes to water." I have some choice words for those labels. While this advice is meant to simplify watering, it ignores how orchids naturally take up water. Orchid roots are designed to be thoroughly soaked and then allowed to dry, mimicking intermittent, yet frequent tropical rains, mixed with plenty of airflow. Ice cubes melt slowly, providing cold water unevenly and never truly flushing the pot. Cold water can also shock orchid roots, and most plants prefer lukewarm or room-temperature water.

Plus, have you ever seen an orchid get watered by an ice cube in nature? If so, can you tell me the brand of those ice cubes because I'd love to buy some.

Myth #5: Get a spider plant; it'll purify the air! But wait . . . do they actually do that?
We've heard this time and time again: Having houseplants is beneficial to your space because they clean harmful chemicals from the air. While it is true that some plants can filter chemicals from the air, the extent of this benefit is often exaggerated. This belief originated with a NASA study in 1989, which examined plants' ability to absorb airborne chemicals in sealed laboratories, not in real homes.

Many studies since have proven this study to be misunderstood. The air-purifying effects of houseplants in typical indoor environments are minimal. To make a meaningful difference in indoor air quality, you would need an impractical number of plants, we're talking thousands of plants in a small square footage area. In most homes, normal airflow, open doors, and ventilation dilute any measurable impact plants might have on those airborne toxins.

5

Creating a Plant-Filled Home

A home filled with plants isn't just about beauty; it brings life into a space. It brings harmony. It is bright and energizing. It adds texture and warmth to a corner. Pairing a plant with a cool planter creates living art. Every season brings a new rhythm, a subtle shift in energy, light, and care. Our plants change with the seasons, and when we learn to move with those shifts instead of against them, our home becomes a living reflection of the natural world.

Back when I was a twosome in my home, we made an agreement. I would contain my indoor jungle to a designated area of the house. My honey's idea of living among the foliage was not exactly his dream aesthetic. In the spirit of compromise, one of the spare bedrooms became my official plant room. It grew into a space where I could do whatever my heart desired. And I did. I filled every square inch with plants, shelves, and grow lights so bright you could probably see the glow from the moon. It was my little space, tucked safely behind a door.

Now, did I quietly let a few plants wander into the shared living spaces? Absolutely. A pothos here, a monstera there—nothing too alarming. But when my life shifted from a twosome to a onesome, everything changed. Once I found my footing again and had the emotional energy to care for plants again, they no longer stayed confined. Slowly at first, then all at once, I began weaving plants

There *IS* such a thing as having too many houseplants.

throughout the entire house. Windowsills, corners, countertops—no space was safe. And if I'm being completely honest, a lot of it was fueled by spite. Grief has a funny way of showing up in unexpected forms, and for me, it came with leaves.

You probably already know the stages of grief:

- Denial
- Anger
- Bargaining
- Depression
- Acceptance

Some people cry. Some people journal. I cried a lot and then I bought more plants.

In the denial stage, I told myself everything was fine and added greenery wherever I could. In the anger stage, I filled the house to the brim. Every empty space now had a plant sitting on top of it. The bargaining stage looked like me convincing myself that just one more plant would make it all feel better. The depression stage came quietly, when even watering felt heavy. And then acceptance arrived slowly, when I realized that plants weren't meant to fill the void, but instead, they were meant to walk alongside me as I healed.

Anger was one of my core grief stages during the beginning. "Fine, you're not here, so I'm filling the entire house with plants." And I did. I was in full panic mode, trying to collect them all. What I learned during that era was that, as much as I absolutely love plants, I do not love feeling overwhelmed by too many things around me. It quickly became a distraction from everything else in my life. I felt a constant pull to check soil, wipe leaves, water, repot, rearrange; care that was once grounding started to feel consuming. The plants that were meant to bring me peace were quietly adding pressure.

Over time, I realized that balance mattered more than volume. At this stage of my plant journey, I'm far more intentional. I focus on a curated collection with thoughtful pops of nature rather than filling every available surface. I keep my bedroom minimal and calm, while larger, more established plants

live in the common areas—plants that don't ask for daily attention and can go longer between waterings.

Plants that need more hands-on attention live where my life naturally passes through, spaces I see every day, so care feels integrated rather than forced. I still have a dedicated plant room and an office that houses many of my favorites in a cabinet, but even those spaces are designed with intention, not excess. This shift taught me something bigger than plant care. Nurturing something doesn't mean overwhelming yourself in the process. And that realization leads me straight into a very controversial topic.

We fall in and out of love with them over time, and that's completely normal. Sometimes we grow frustrated with plants when we see pests. I can't tell you how many times, over my years of growing, I've looked at a leaf covered in thrips and briefly envisioned chucking my entire plant collection into an open flame. Dramatic? Maybe. Relatable? Absolutely. Having a large plant collection is a full-time job in itself. It leaves very little room to slack on plant care and can quickly become overwhelming, especially if you're also wearing other hats in life: parent, employee, partner, caregiver, or all of the above. Plants don't pause when life gets busy. They still need water, light, observation, and attention, even when your schedule feels maxed out. This is why I'm so intentional about how I talk about plant care. My mission has always been to help people grow confidence and to appreciate plants for their beauty—not to promote the idea that more plants somehow equals more success. The size of your collection does *not* determine how skilled, dedicated, or "qualified" you are as a plant parent.

Integrating Plants into the Home

We're plant lovers—of course we want to feel more connected to nature while we're inside our homes. Plants are more than just decoration. They are companionship, connection, and care. A home filled with plants feels alive. Nature isn't something you visit just when you're outside, but something you live alongside every day.

Your home is your tropical getaway, your sanctuary, and the plants you choose should reflect your personality. Are you a maximalist who dreams of a wild indoor jungle? Are you a minimalist that prefers a more organized jungle with statement pieces? There's no wrong way to fill your home with plants, but being purposeful can make a difference.

Follow the Light

Before setting up your plant space, take time to truly assess your environment. As we talked about in chapter 4, remember *all* plants need sunlight to grow—there's no way around that. One of the most important first steps is understanding how far your intended plant space is from a window. Distance matters just as much as window size. From there, if you're working with natural light, note which direction your window faces and pay attention to when and how sunlight moves through the space throughout the day. Light can change in intensity, color, or distribution over time, and observing it helps you make informed choices instead of guessing.

In my living room, I have a perfect little cove that practically begged for plants. Visually, it was ideal, but the reality was less ideal. That space sits about 20 feet (6 m) away from a north-facing window. Big womp. Instead of forcing low-light plants to survive there, I leaned into a solution that made sense—grow lights. Choosing to supplement with lighting allowed me to build the plant wall I had been imagining without compromising plant health.

Because this wall is a main focal point in my home, aesthetics mattered just as much as function. I opted for warm-bulb grow lights so the space still felt cozy and inviting rather than stark or clinical.

Think Beyond Your Average Pots

Consider wall-mounted planters, hanging baskets, trailing vines on shelves, a grow cabinet, or a lush terrarium centerpiece. Plants don't have to be confined to windowsills, so don't be afraid to integrate your nooks with different setups.

previous Lush greenery fills a vertical shelf from floor to ceiling. A mix of trailing vines, tropical plants, and climbing foliage creates layers of texture and movement, all anchored by baskets, shelves, and a wall grid that doubles as both support and décor. A warm pendant light with a grow bulb illuminates the plants, blending function with ambiance, while neutral walls allow the greens to stand out.

a workspace plant setup

Studies show that having plants in your workspace can improve productivity and mood, and even reduce stress. In case you were looking for a sign to buy more plants, this is your sign. A trailing philodendron, a small cactus, or a tabletop terrarium with a lamp on your desk can make all the difference.

Lush greenery fills a vertical shelf from floor to ceiling. A mix of trailing vines, tropical plants, and climbing foliage creates layers of texture and movement, all anchored by baskets, shelves, and a wall grid that doubles as both support and décor. A warm pendant light with a grow bulb illuminates the plants, blending function with ambiance, while neutral walls allow the greens to stand out.

Style Plants at Different Heights

One of the fastest ways to make a plant-filled home feel intentional (and not cluttered) is to style plants at varying heights. In nature, plants don't all live at the same level. In your home, mimicking those growth patterns by mixing floor plants, tabletop plants, eye-level plants, and overhead greenery creates depth, movement, and a sense of flow throughout a space.

Think in layers by using tall floor plants to anchor the room, medium plants to fill in shelves and plant stands, and trailing plants to soften edges around windows and vertical décor elements. This approach allows you to add more plants without overwhelming the room while also giving each one its moment to shine.

Add Floating Shelves and Hang Plants from the Ceiling

Running out of shelf space? Go vertical! Floating shelves are one of the easiest ways to bring plants into unused vertical space. They're perfect for any sized home, or anyone wanting a clean, modern look without adding bulky furniture. Floating shelves draw the eye upward, create visual interest, and lift plants closer to light sources like windows or grow lights, while keeping countertops and floors clear instead of overcrowded.

With that being said, watering logistics matter. If something isn't in my direct line of vision, I forget it exists. Add in the fact that I'm part of the *fun-size crew* at 4'11" (1.5 m), and suddenly every high shelf requires a ladder. To make vertical setups sustainable, I plan ahead by using drip trays or cache pots

Integrate unique shelves to make use of window space, especially when windows are limited. In my attempt to avoid making more holes in my walls and having more shelves take up floor space, I found a shelf that latches onto the window sill while still allowing my window to close.

to catch excess water, choosing plants that can tolerate longer dry cycles, or placing the highest plants in self-watering pots that I only have to refill occasionally. Vertical plant styling should feel inspiring, not stressful, so designing it with accessibility in mind ensures those plants stay healthy long after the shelves go up.

How to style them:

- Choose lightweight planters and secure ceiling hooks properly.
- Stick with trailing plants like pothos, philodendrons, spider plants (*Chlorophytum comosum*), or string-of-things plants.
- Hang plants at staggered heights for a layered look.
- Make sure they're still accessible for watering and care.
- Place them near bright windows, but avoid direct, harsh sun unless the plant prefers it.

Creating a Perfect Balance: Design and Care

A plant-filled home doesn't have to mean stuffing every corner with greenery; it's about being intentional with which plant babies live with you. Also remember, your space will evolve and grow more lush with time, so keep that in mind when you're planning your positioning.

Here are two of my best design tips to keep in mind.

Tip #1: Consider the space you're working with and find one focal point to build around.

- Let the larger plants be the star of the room: *Monstera deliciosa*, *Ficus* spp., bird of paradise (*Strelitzia reginae*), and split-leaf philodendron (*Philodendron bipinnatifidum*) are examples of plants that will quickly take over the space they live in and will be your anchor pieces.
- Layer mid-height plants (snake plants, *Dracaena* spp., philodendrons) to fill visual gaps.
- Incorporate smaller plants around, creating your own indoor ecosystem.
- Add trailing plants (pothos, string of hearts, orchids) on shelves for whimsy and softness.
- For a calming, cohesive vibe, keep your pots within a similar color palette. Think terracotta warmth, neutral whites, or earthy greens. Or for a fun and quirky setup, use colorful, bright-colored mismatched pots.

Tip #2: Create a unique setup where you can integrate smaller plants with less maintenance.

- A living wall or a bioactive terrarium is a great way to showcase various plants. Not only is it a great conversation starter, but by having many plants in one space, it makes caring for them easier.
- A simpler way to modify a cabinet is by switching out glass shelves for acrylic shelves. Acrylic shelves are available online for purchase with different designs and cutouts for airflow. Grow lights are a staple in a cabinet for healthy plants, along with small fans to keep the temperature comfortable yet free from fungal issues in an enclosed space.

In this modified grow cabinet, I house my smaller hoyas, smaller anthuriums, and a few variegated plants that benefit from more controlled conditions. The cabinet allows me to provide consistent light, higher humidity if I want, and stable temperatures—all things these plants appreciate, especially as they establish and grow. It also gives me a way to group plants with similar needs together, simplifying care while managing a diverse collection.

above A large terrarium, like the one shown here, should have grow lights set on a timer to provide consistent, reliable light throughout the day. The initial building took a full week, but the maintenance is minimal. A fogger or misting system can also be automated, making watering and humidity control a breeze. While these systems take a lot of the daily guesswork out of care, regular maintenance is still important. Opening the doors for a few minutes each week allows for fresh airflow, helps regulate humidity, and prevents plants from overgrowing or developing issues related to stagnant air.

opposite I also like to go into my cabinet terrarium with a spray bottle every other week to ensure the moss stays evenly damp, especially in areas the misting system may not reach. Incorporating springtails and isopods introduces a built-in cleanup crew that helps break down waste and decaying plant matter, recycling nutrients back into the system. Together, these elements create a mostly self-sustaining ecosystem. It's one that thrives on balance, simple observations, and small, intentional check-ins rather than constant hands-on care.

Grow Plants That Thrive in Your Conditions, Don't Change Your Conditions to Grow Plants

As I was growing my own collection and feeling a bit overwhelmed by the different care needs of all the different plants I had, it hit me—grow plants that will thrive in your conditions rather than changing your conditions to grow plants.

I think about it much like when I trained my dog Pablo at eight weeks old. When I brought him home, I was already deep into my plant jungle lifestyle. I worried about him chewing on something harmful, but I also knew it wasn't realistic, or fair, to completely strip my home of the plants I loved. Some of them were simply too large, too established, and part of the shared spaces in my home. Instead of changing the environment out of fear, I chose to teach within it.

I left the plants where they lived and introduced Pablo to them the same way I introduced him to everything else in my home. When he got curious and put his nose too deep into the soil or tried to take a nibble, I gently redirected him to something more appropriate, like a toy. With time and consistency, he learned. The plants became a part of the background, no more interesting than a chair or a table. I had done the same with my other dog, Maxi, years earlier, using the same calm, patient approach.

Just like Pablo and Maxi learned the rhythms of my home, so did my plants. Once I stopped forcing them to fit into unrealistic expectations, everything settled into balance. The plants I chose thrived when I stopped asking them to be something they weren't meant to be.

This shift changed everything for me. My collection became more resilient, more joyful, and far more reflective of who I am and how I live. And that's what I want for you, too. Not a house full of high-maintenance plants that leave you feeling behind, but a collection that supports your lifestyle, your well-being, and your confidence as a plant parent. You're choosing sustainability over stress. You're building a collection that can weather change, new routines, new homes, new priorities.

Light will always be number one, and making sure you have the proper setup to sustain your plants is a given. Adding grow lights to a space is easy enough but when you feel like you need to add humidifiers and grow tents to be able to fully enjoy your collection, I find that can easily lead to plant burnout if your lifestyle changes for any reason.

One of the ways I've been able to accomplish this is by sticking to general

Plants can get used to the rhythm of your home and your care in much the same way a pet, like my dog Pablo, does.

species of plants that fit my lifestyle. I travel for pleasure, but I also travel for work. If leaving my plants for a week would cause me to stress over the fear of my collection going to ruins, then I know this lifestyle would no longer be sustainable for me. Sticking to plants that can easily bounce back from longer periods of dryness felt like a happy balance. As much as I love the look of alocasias (*Alocasia* spp.), not only do they drop leaves with any care inconsistencies, but they also require frequent monitoring and consistent treatments to keep them free from pests like spider mites. For a season of my life, I did try to make it work. I told myself that if I just adjusted one more thing—one more humidifier, one more treatment—I could keep them happy. But over time, I realized I was adjusting *my life* far more than the plants were adjusting to me and my environment.

That realization was freeing. Keeping it simple has continued to fuel my passion for my plant collection because it's not very difficult to keep up. Instead of forcing myself into a version of plant care that felt rigid and demanding, I began choosing plants that aligned with how I already lived: Plants that didn't panic if I missed a watering and plants that didn't unravel if humidity dipped for a few days became my go-to ones.

I leaned into thicker foliage plants like hoyas, snake plants, pothos, even philodendrons, and they became the backbone of my collection. Not because they were trendy or "easy," but because they were resilient. Knowing what I know about myself and my plant care abilities, when I want to go into a genus of plants that is absolutely beautiful but a little more on the thirsty side, I know I will have to look into changing the substrate to one able to hold more moisture longer and incorporate a self-watering pot.

Find the plants you enjoy growing the most, ones that can truly thrive in your space and support you in your current lifestyle—not the lifestyle you think you *should* have, but the one you're actually living right now.

right My collection of African violets lives in small, self-watering pots with a wick to maintain moisture consistently. Wicking pots work by using capillary action, where a wick draws water up from a bottom reservoir into the soil as the soil dries, providing a consistent supply of water to the roots. Once the reservoir contains no water, refill again to just below the pot's base (but not touching it).

opposite I keep plants like begonias in my enclosed terrarium, or I have them in a substrate called Pon (a soil alternative normally combined with lava rock, pumice, and/or zeolite) that I use instead of regular chunky soil mix. Another adjustment I've made is that I have my peace lily growing in Leca (lightweight expanded clay aggregate; a.k.a. clay balls).

I decided I wanted a statement plant piece to be able to house high humidity-loving plants, so I converted a cabinet into a terrarium where I could showcase these plants in a cool way, and their maintenance would be minimal. Inside, I have at least thirty different plants like begonias (*Begonia* spp.), anthuriums, orchids, and alocasias. The fogger system keeps the terrarium damp and all I have to do is fill the fogger system with water biweekly and spray down any of the sphagnum moss approximately once a week if needed.

what to do if you need to simplify your collection

Owning plants, especially when owning a larger collection, will result in moments where you are at the peak of caring for them. But there will also be moments when you're ready to physically slow down, and when you see a wilted and thirsty plant that needs to be watered or a plant that needs to be treated for pests, you might feel like crawling into a hole.

Our tastes and capacities change too. You may realize certain plants no longer excite you the way they once did, or that your lifestyle has shifted and you're craving something simpler, sturdier, or lower maintenance. If at any point plant care begins to feel anxiety-inducing, overwhelming, or like something you're actively avoiding, especially when it pulls you away from rest, connection, or time spent out in the world, that's often a signal to pause and reevaluate. Plants are meant to enhance your life, not quietly drain you.

There are many ways to simplify without giving everything up. Combining plants with similar care needs into the same pot can reduce maintenance while still creating fullness and visual appeal. Choosing fewer, more resilient plants can restore balance. And if downsizing feels like the right choice, know that it isn't giving up; you're taking the time to find balance and clarity again. We thrive best when our environments reflect what we genuinely have the capacity to care for.

Tips for downsizing your collection:

1. You can gift them to friends or family.

2. Donate them to local places. Many spaces are great for plants, such as:

- Schools or classrooms
- Libraries
- Community centers
- Churches and other nonprofits
- Local shelters

Just be sure to call ahead first to confirm.

3. Sell them locally. Places include:

- Facebook Marketplace
- Local plant swap groups
- Neighborhood apps
- Garage sales or pop-ups

4. Offer them to local plant shops. Some independent nurseries:

- Accept donations
- Take plants for store credit
- Rehome rehab plants

5. Compost (when appropriate). Compost plants that are:

- Severely declining
- Pest-infested (after proper disposal)
- Beyond saving

6. Downsize slowly. You don't have to do it all at once.

- One shelf at a time
- One room at a time
- One decision per week

Keeping Your Plants in Harmony Year-Round

Like our plants, we too adapt to the seasons. As for me, during the spring and summer I am at what I consider my best. I am upbeat, I am ready to take on new activities, I long for summer adventures, and I feel energized by the sun. I thrive in the warmth. I am living out my garden-fairy fantasies when harvesting my veggies, picking flowers, and admiring the ecosystem filled with the bees, birds, and bunnies I've welcomed to my backyard. My feet are bare on the grass every chance I get. I am grounded. During the fall and winter though, I slow down drastically. My energy level shifts inward. The seasonal sadness shows up to my front door. My mood changes. I spend more time reflecting and nurturing the energy I have left. I cozy up indoors, anticipate changes, and prune what doesn't serve me in preparation for new growth.

We are just like plants, but with more complicated emotions.

For our plants, too, every season brings a new rhythm, a subtle shift in energy, light, and care. When you learn to move with those shifts instead of against them, your home becomes a living reflection of the natural world—adaptable, balanced, alive, and ready for its next phase of growth. In order to be successful with our houseplants through all seasons, we too must change our routines to reflect their growth patterns and needs.

Spring—the Season of Renewal

Spring is energy in motion. Everything awakens. Roots stretch, leaves unfurl, and growth begins again. You'll notice your plants responding almost instantly with brighter colors, faster growth, and new leaves unfurling overnight. It's their season of possibility and the start of change.

Krystal's Tips for Spring:

- Prepare soil mixes so you're ready for repotting and top-offs.
- Stock up on fertilizers and pest treatments before growth really takes off.
- Refresh old and tired potting soil by replacing the top inch (3 cm) with a fresh mix to boost nutrients.
- Wash watering cans and sprayers to start the season clean and pest-free.

Nature never hurries and never resists change. It adjusts in its own time, quietly and with purpose.

- Prune away dead or damaged leaves to encourage healthy new growth.
- Begin fertilizing lightly for all plants as they "wake up" and resume active growth.
- Repot root-bound plants to give them new space to grow.
- Clean your windows to maximize sunlight from the return of brighter, longer days.
- If you're up for it, gradually transition bright light–loving plants outdoors into shaded areas to acclimate them safely (see next section).

Moving plants outdoors

For optimum growth, I bring many of my houseplants outdoors during the warmer months. Now, keep in mind that I live in Indiana, where we get all four seasons, so I can only keep them outside during the spring and summer. I will say that this process can be a stressful one, but the growth of the plants is well worth it for me.

I want to acknowledge the process of this transition. It can be tedious if you're not prepared. Now if you're asking yourself, "Why go through this process in the first place if it's a tedious one?" Well, for me, a few weeks of sweat in exchange for booming growth and vibrant colors is well worth it. It's also a good time to check the basics. Outdoor conditions dry the soil faster, the air pulls moisture from leaves, and rain doesn't always replace watering, especially if your temps and weather are as inconsistent as mine are here in Indiana. What worked indoors may need to be adjusted for life on the outside.

Every year I set up my bright light-loving cacti in their own display that I've coined "The Beef Bar." Why beef bar? I started the nickname "beef" for my cacti many years ago when I saw the largest saguaro cactus *Carnegiea gigantea* in Acapulco, Mexico. The names of many cacti have never been easy for me to pronounce, so in my excitement, I yelled out "That's a big beef!" and the nickname has stuck ever since.

First, you will become the greatest weather person during this transition. I don't make the transition until the nighttime temperature outside is consistently above 55°F (13°C), and I wait until the final frost date has passed. Bringing houseplants out sooner can result in leaf damage or worse—a cold plant death. Next, decide which plants you like to bring out.

Here are some things to consider:

1. Do I have a shaded or protected area to start the acclimation process?

2. Will I have the space for it indoors if the plant booms with growth during its time outdoors?

3. How awful is it going to be to clean up the cobwebs and other critters that have made these plants their home when I'm ready to move them back indoors in the fall?

4. Am I willing to take the risk of this plant not making it outdoors due to leaf burn and the elements?

5. Does this plant actually benefit from stronger light, or is it already thriving indoors?

6. Can I easily move this plant in and out during the transition period if the weather shifts suddenly?

7. Am I prepared to water more frequently once it's outside?

8. Will upcoming travel or busy weeks interfere with proper care?

Since I have a collection of over 300 houseplants, I chose to move the plants I know will thrive with more bright light than they receive inside. I move all my ficus, bird of paradise, succulents, carnivorous plants, and cacti.

Even with the brightest light I can give them indoors (artificial light or sunlight), this still is no match for outdoor sunlight. That being said . . .

Please do not place your houseplants in direct outdoor sunlight without a transition period.

Even just a few minutes of direct sunlight without a gradual transition will scorch the leaves to infinity and beyond. Even for desert plants, it is so important to gradually transition them from indoors to outdoors.

The Beef Bar, with my collection of cactus, consists of cinderblocks stacked on the sides with cedar planks stacked on top. All of my prickly babies get transitioned from inside to outside after the last frost date passes. I slowly transition them to full sun over time by first putting them on the west-facing side of my home about two weeks then moving them to The Beef Bar. Having a designated place for them to receive the bright light they thrive in makes caring for them easier and they bloom consistently.

Start by placing the plants outside in the shade for a few hours per day, then work your way up to a full twenty-four-hour period. If you can, place them in a spot that protects them from harsh elements like wind, strong sunlight, and rain, perhaps under a porch or awning. After a week, any desert plants, like cacti and succulents, can graduate from the shade to direct sunlight, but start with a few hours of direct sunlight per day and work your way up to a full day.

This process of "hardening" will take at least two weeks. It's something I do every spring, and although I yell throughout the whole process as I move the pots, seeing all their eventual growth brings so much joy.

Summer—the Season of Expansion

Summer is the season of warmth, fullness, and vitality. Your plants will drink more water, soak in more light, and grow with more oomph.

But too much of a good thing can also overwhelm. This is when balance becomes key—giving your plants what they need without overdoing it.

Krystal's Tips for Summer

- You may find yourself watering more often, but observe your plants carefully. Heat increases evaporation, yet overwatering can still happen if soil doesn't dry properly.
- Check pots and drainage holes to ensure water can escape easily during heavy summer waterings. Soggy roots are one of the quickest ways to stress a plant and cause rot.
- Expect faster growth and be ready to support it with stakes, trellises, or moss poles as plants stretch toward the light.
- Use sheer curtains to soften harsh sunlight coming through windows.
- Increase airflow with fans or open windows when possible, to help prevent pests and fungal issues during warmer, more humid days.
- Keep an eye out for pests, as summer warmth can cause pests to multiply quickly. Early detection makes all the difference.

Summer is also a time to enjoy your home and the plants you've nurtured. Host dinners near your greenery, propagate cuttings to share with friends (see page 143), and fill your space with gratitude for how far everything has come—including you!

Although in nature most ficus species grow as large trees in direct sunlight outdoors, when we grow them as houseplants—and especially when we move them outside for the summer—they need to go through a gradual transition. Indoor light, even in a bright window, is far gentler than outdoor sun. Without acclimation, leaves can scorch quickly, leading to sunburn and unnecessary stress. My ficus live outside on my porch during the spring and summer, where they receive a few hours of soft morning light followed by shade for the rest of the day. This slow introduction allows their leaves to toughen up and adapt to increased light levels without damage. Over time, they grow stronger, fuller, and more resilient. This ease in their transition makes all the difference between a stressed plant and a thriving one.

The Beef Bar is brought back inside for the colder months. They live on a shelf system I created using stacked wooden crates and PVC plastic cut down to size. It's simple, functional, and sturdy enough to support the weight of heavier pots. The setup gives them height, airflow, and clear visibility, which is key for keeping an eye on watering needs during winter.

Fall—the Season of Grounding

Fall slows things down. Light fades earlier, growth softens, and your plants begin preparing for rest. Leaves may drop, watering needs change, and what once felt like constant growth begins to quiet down.

Krystal's Tips for Fall

- Check in with your watering routine. With cooler temperatures and less light, soil stays moist longer. You may have to adjust your watering according to new environmental conditions now that the season has changed.
- If plants are slowing down in growth, slow down with fertilizing them. If they're still growing strong, continue fertilizing.
- Take time to clean dust from leaves and inspect for pests before winter arrives. This small step can prevent bigger issues later on.
- Combine plants you have multiples of, or that have similar care, to save space and simplify your routine.
- Pay attention to drafts from windows and doors as temperatures fluctuate, and move sensitive plants away from cold air.

Fall feels like nature gently reminding us to slow down and take stock of what we've grown. It's a season of grounding, releasing what no longer serves us, and making space for rest. Just as plants pull their energy inward, we're likely to do the same.

Vacation's over: transitioning plants back indoors

As summer begins to wind down and the cold air starts to raise the hairs on the back of your neck, you know what that means—hello, fall! It's time to start paying close attention to nighttime temperatures. Keep that weather app open, friends, because you will be checking the forecast countless times during this transition. While many tropical houseplants enjoy their summer vacation outdoors, most are not built to handle cool evenings. As a general rule, once nighttime temperatures consistently dip below 55°F to 60°F (13°C to 16°C), it's time to begin the move back inside. This transition should happen well before the first frost is even on the forecast. Frost damage happens quickly and sometimes invisibly at first, showing up days later as blackened or mushy leaves. Trust me, waiting "just one more night" is often how damage happens.

moving plants back inside: what's normal vs. what's a problem

Normal acclimation responses:

- Dropping a few older or lower leaves
- Mild yellowing as light levels decrease
- Slower or no growth
- Temporary wilting after relocation
- Smaller new leaves forming indoors

Signs of a problem:

- Rapid or excessive leaf drop across the entire plant
- Blackened, mushy, or translucent leaves (often signs of cold or frost damage)
- Persistent wilting despite moist soil
- Widespread yellowing combined with soggy soil (overwatering)
- Sudden pest outbreaks after moving indoors

Before bringing plants indoors, take time to inspect them closely. Outdoor living often comes with hitchhikers: spider mites, thrips, ants, or other insects that would love to move indoors with your plants. A blast of water from the hose to the leaves and stems helps to dislodge them, and remember my DIY cleaning spray from page 75? Keep that handy for this because you'll be doing a lot of leaf cleaning during this process.

Start by removing any damaged or dying foliage. This can go a long way in easing the transition. Also, the top few inches of soil can become home to unwanted indoor "friends," so gently remove 1 to 2 inches (3 to 5 cm) from the top of the soil to reduce these unwanted hitchhikers and limit the risk of indoor pest outbreaks. Replace the removed soil with fresh, new soil to the same level.

Once the plant is inside, consider whether it will be returning to a space with less natural light than it had outdoors. Many plants benefit from supplemental grow lights, especially in the early weeks indoors, to reduce the shock of less daylight. Even placing plants closer to windows than they will live for the rest of the winter months can help them adjust more gradually.

I don't know about you, but I'm a whole different person in the spring and summer

than I am in the fall and winter. During the cold seasons, I am pale, slow moving, and wilted. Plants coming back indoors are not much different, so don't be alarmed if your plants look a little . . . let's say dramatic . . . after the move. Leaves may soon yellow, growth will pause, and everything seems to move at a different pace. This doesn't mean something is wrong; it means your plants are adjusting to their environment and preparing for what comes next.

Winter—the Season of Rest

Winter is the quiet pause. It's the season of patience and reflection. Growth slows, light weakens, and your plants (and you) need gentleness.

Krystal's Tips for Winter

- You may have to adjust your watering in winter. Don't assume watering is the same now as in the fall. If you're running the heat during the winter, the air in your home is likely drier, which can cause plants to dry out faster even though they're growing more slowly. Always check the soil first.
- Move plants closer to windows to maximize limited daylight, or supplement with grow lights to maintain consistent light exposure.
- Protect plants from cold drafts near windows, doors, and vents, as sudden temperature drops can stress leaves and roots. A vent deflector can also be used for any heat vent with nearby plants to change the direction of the hot air.
- Check regularly for pests, especially spider mites. Dry winter air creates the perfect environment for them to thrive. Look for fine webbing, stippled or dusty-looking leaves, dropped leaves, and overall plant decline. Catching them early makes treatment much easier. Wipe leaves down, rinse plants when possible, and increase humidity with a humidifier to help deter them.
- Embrace the stillness. Your plants aren't dying; they're restoring.

Winter asks us to honor rest; to stop striving and simply sustain. We are not meant to be moving as fast as we were in the brighter seasons. This is a time to observe, to care gently, and to trust what we can't yet see. Stillness is a vital part of growth.

Don't be discouraged by fewer leaves or slower growth. This season is building strength beneath the surface.

6

Creative DIY Projects

One indoor jungle is unlike any other. Every time you build something for your plants, whether it be a trellis, a propagation wall, or hanging plant art, you're creating a tropical oasis all your own. The way you showcase your plants will change the way your home functions and flows.

It's easy to buy everything ready-made, but creating something yourself adds a different kind of energy to your home. A handmade propagation station carries the warmth of your effort. A repurposed jar or painted pot becomes uniquely yours. It's a reflection of time, patience, and care. You don't get to overthink when you're doing a plant project. Find your concept, get the materials, and go for it. Nature doesn't worry about straight lines or perfect edges, and neither should you.

Before you run to the store, take a look around your home. That empty candle jar or forgotten vase tucked in a cabinet? It might be the perfect propagation vessel. An old basket collecting dust can instantly be transformed into a hanging planter with a liner and a little creativity. Mason jars, driftwood, twine—these everyday items can become beautiful plant displays when you see them through a different lens.

Some of the most fun I've had with my plants has come from experimenting with how I style them throughout my home. Rearranging, repurposing, and creating new displays keeps things fresh and engaging. The beauty of plants is that there's a

never-ending array of projects we can explore. Create those propagation stations, hanging installations, living art pieces, and small moments of greenery tucked into unexpected places. In this chapter, you'll find a collection of my favorite plant projects. I hope you have as much fun making them as I did.

A polka dot begonia (*Begonia maculata*) cutting displayed in a glass vase. Clear jars allow light to reach the developing roots, which makes it easy to monitor root growth, water clarity, and overall health. This visibility is helpful for beginners and for plants that root quickly, however, light exposure can encourage algae growth, which competes with roots for oxygen. Colored jars limit the amount of light reaching the roots, more closely mimicking how roots grow in nature, and they help reduce algae buildup.

Mystery Propagation Container

Perfect for any plant lover who enjoys a little surprise, a mystery propagation container is a sealed or semi-sealed clear container filled with *unlabeled* plant cuttings that will propagate and eventually be identified as they grow. These containers are incredibly useful for successful propagation. The enclosed environment helps maintain consistent humidity, reducing moisture loss and stress on fresh cuttings while roots develop. This makes them especially helpful for harder-to-root plants or for propagating during drier months.

materials you'll need:

- 3 to 5 healthy plant cuttings (easy propagators like pothos, silver pothos [*Scindapsus pictus*], hoya, monstera, and so on)
- Small clear container with lid
- Perlite or sphagnum moss (to anchor the cuttings and keep them hydrated
- Spray bottle with water
- A "care card" with general propagation tips

1

2

3

1. **Choose your cuttings.** Take stem cuttings of beginner-friendly plants that root easily. Good options include:
    - Pothos
    - Philodendron
    - Tradescantias
    - Hoya
    - Scindapsus
    - Syngonium

2. **Fill the container with the growing medium.** Pour in a few inches of perlite or sphagnum moss.

    Ideas for containers:

    - Recycled glass jars
    - Takeout soup containers
    - Acrylic boxes with a lid

3. **Add the cuttings to the container.** Carefully place your cuttings into the mystery container, inserting their cut base into the growing medium.

4

5

4. Add water. Use a spray bottle filled with fresh water to hydrate the growing medium and then close the lid.

5. Include a care card. On a small card or printed sheet, add general propagation instructions (light, water, patience!)

Aftercare: Pot up the cuttings into soil when their roots are 1 to 2 inches (3 to 5 cm) long and preferably when they show secondary roots growing from the main root.

above Don't be afraid to experiment with using other propagation mediums. Shown here as a propagation medium is Pon. Pon is typically a blend of pumice stone, lava rock, and zeolite. The clear container allows light in while maintaining humidity, creating an ideal environment for cuttings to root and thrive. Inside, small plant starts are neatly arranged, showing early root development and fresh growth.

Pingdom/Bog Bowl

No, this is not a dog bowl—it's a bog bowl! This bowl is a way to bring the bog from outside to inside by creating a miniature wetland ecosystem right in your home. In this creepy little bowl, you'll house some seriously cool carnivorous plants that thrive in consistently moist conditions. When deciding which carnivorous plants to use, it's best to choose species that do *not* require a winter dormancy period. While Venus flytraps and pitcher plants (*Sarracenia* spp.) are iconic, they need dormancy, which means you'd eventually have to remove them from the bowl as winter approaches. To keep things simple and beginner-friendly, opt for plants that are happy growing year-round indoors.

Great starter options include *Pinguicula* spp., also known as pings or butterworts (hence the project name of Pingdom!), and cape sundew (*Drosera capensis*). Both are forgiving, visually interesting, and excellent at trapping tiny insects.

materials you'll need:

- Container with no drainage holes (preferably plastic, glass, or glazed ceramic)
- Substrate: Use a nutrient-free mix. Combine approximately one part perlite with two parts peat moss. You also need to cut small bits of dampened long-fiber sphagnum moss and incorporate it into the mix for water retention.
- Distilled water, rainwater, or reverse osmosis water. Carnivorous plants require water that is low in minerals. Tap water, well water, and bottled water will kill most carnivorous plants.
- **Optional:** Lava rock or dragon stone to use as decoration, and live moss or sheet moss.

1

2

1. **Wet the substrate.** Start by lightly dampening your substrate with distilled, rain, or reverse-osmosis water until it feels evenly moist but not sopping wet. Add the mix to your container, gently pressing it down just enough to remove large air pockets. Bog plants thrive in soft, airy soil conditions.

2. **Place the plants.** Create small planting pockets and carefully place your carnivorous plants into the mix. Handle them gently, especially the roots, and position each plant so the crown sits just above the soil surface.

3. **Dress with moss.** Once planted, lightly top-dress with a thin layer of moss. This helps retain moisture, keeps the surface tidy, and mimics the bog natural habitat. Use a small brush to clean off any substate that has fallen on top of the sticky leaves.

4. **Water.** Water your bog bowl by slowly pouring water around the edges until the substrate is fully saturated. Because this container has no drainage holes, avoid overfilling—your goal is a consistently moist soil, not standing water above the surface.

Aftercare: Place your bog bowl in bright light, or under a grow light for twelve to fourteen hours a day. These plants love light, and adequate lighting is key to vibrant color and healthy growth. With these small carnivorous babies, you'll know they're happy when the sundews sparkle with sticky dew and the butterwort leaves feel slightly tacky to the touch.

From there, maintenance is simple. Keep the substrate moist at all times using only approved water sources, avoid fertilizing, and let your plants do what they do best—grow slowly and beautifully, and help manage those pesky gnats along the way.

A bog bowl isn't just a project; it's a tiny ecosystem. One that reminds us that sometimes the most fascinating worlds come together in the smallest, neatest little bowls.

Tropical pitcher plants (*Nepenthes*) can also work in a bog bowl setup, but they prefer to dry slightly in-between waterings, so placement and moisture control are important considerations.

Mini Hanging Kokedama

Styling plants is an artform all in itself and seldom more so than when creating kokedama. The name *kokedama* in Japanese translates to "koke" meaning moss and "dama" meaning ball. These living moss spheres are part of centuries-old tradition in Japanese gardening and can be displayed resting on a decorative surface or suspended by string in front of a window. Kokedama is both plant care and design—an intentional way to showcase plants while mimicking how they might naturally grow in the wild.

Traditionally, kokedama is made using *akadama* or bonsai soil, a clay-based medium that holds moisture well and supports root structure. In this version, however, the moss ball is placed inside an enclosed dome. The dome creates a consistently humid microclimate, allowing the moss and plant to stay hydrated for longer periods with minimal intervention. This makes it more forgiving for beginners while still honoring the essence of the technique.

materials you'll need:

- Glass dome
- Small suction cup
- A small plant. Good options are ferns, pothos, begonias, or jewel orchids (*Ludisia discolor*)
- Moss (sheet moss, long-fiber sphagnum moss, or live moss)
- Clear fishing line, twine, or jute string
- Scissors
- Water
- Gloves (optional but helpful)

1

2

1. **Prepare the plant.** Choose your plant and remove the soil. Shape the moss into a ball and insert the bare roots of the plant into the moss.
2. **Wrap with more moss and shape it into a tight ball.**

3

4

3. Tie the ball together. Secure the ball by wrapping it with fishing line pulled tightly. Continue to shape by trimming the moss as needed.

4. Hang it up. Hang the finished ball up inside the dome with fishing line secured to a small suction cup inside the top of the dome.

Note: If you choose to skip hanging it in a glass dome, incorporate bonsai soil or akadama inside the moss ball after step 1.

Aftercare: Although your kokedama ball will maintain moisture much longer being enclosed, water your kokedama regularly by soaking it in a small bowl of water for five to ten minutes or until it feels heavy. Repeat whenever the ball feels light and the moss is dry. Fertilize every few weeks with a water-soluble fertilizer in the water bowl. If the plant has grown large and roots have started growing out of the moss, it may be time to move the plant to a larger ball.

Air Dry Clay Flower Frog

Some of the best gifts I've received are the ones that are homemade. There's something deeply meaningful about knowing someone took the time to create something by hand. I love the idea of sharing plants with others and presenting them in a way that can be used for many years to come. A flower frog is not only a beautiful way to style and share plant propagations, but it's also incredibly practical. You can make them any size to fit any vessel, customize the shape and color to match your aesthetic, and use them for fresh-cut flowers or plant propagations just as easily. This DIY project is perfect for beginners and doesn't require special tools. The majority of the items used you can find lying around your home, making it perfect for a cozy afternoon craft.

materials you'll need:

- Air dry clay in the terracotta color
- Rolling pin
- Clay round hole cutter
- Waterproof sealant
- Jar/glass vessel
- Plant cuttings

1

2

3

1. **Roll clay into a ball.**

2. **Roll clay evenly** out to a thickness of about ¼ inch (6 mm).

3. **Cut out a circle—**I used a mason jar lid as a template.

4. **Create the scalloped edges.**

5. **Cut out the holes** and let the clay dry; this sat overnight to dry.

6. **Seal with a waterproof glaze.** Let the glaze dry and place it on top of the jar filled with water and insert the plant cuttings. You are ready to use or gift to a friend.

Aftercare: Each flower frog becomes one of a kind, carrying the marks of the hands that made it. Long after the cuttings have rooted or the flowers have faded, the flower frog remains; making it a reusable, thoughtful piece that encourages creativity, sustainability, and connection through plants.

4

5

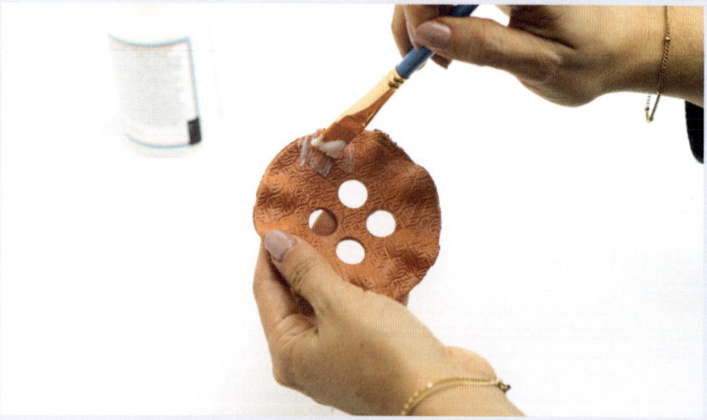

6

materials you'll need:

- Mini orchid
- Driftwood or cork bark
- Cotton wick; about 6 inches (15 cm) long
- Damp sphagnum moss
- Sheet moss or live moss
- Clear fishing line, twine, or jute string
- Plastic reservoir
- 2 screws or 2 small nails
- Hanging hook

Self-Watering Mini Hanging Orchid

Oh, orchids, how I love you so! Yet so misunderstood and looked at as difficult plants, when in reality, they do a wonderful job at communicating their needs in their own quiet, planty ways. Once you learn how to read them—the color of their roots, the firmness of their leaves, the rhythm of their growth—they become some of the most rewarding plants to care for.

This project showcases an orchid growing how it would in nature—elevated, airy, and on display while still being practical for everyday life. It includes a self-watering setup with a water reservoir and a wicking system to provide the orchid with consistent water.

This mini hanging orchid not only turns the plant into living art, but it also removes much of the intimidation around orchid care. It's a reminder that when we design plant setups that work *with* a plant's natural habits instead of against them, caring for them becomes simpler and far more enjoyable.

1

2

3

4

1. **Prepare the roots.** Remove the orchid from its current substate and remove all substrate. Trim and thin any dying roots.

2. **Place the orchid.**Position the orchid in the middle of the driftwood or piece of cork bark, along with the cotton wick, in the middle.

3. **Wrap sphagnum moss around the roots of the orchid.**

4. **Secure with fishing line.** Wrap fishing line, twine, or string around the whole thing repeatedly over the root mass while pulling semi-tightly to secure the orchid roots and their moss covering to the driftwood or cork bark.

5

6

5. **Add more moss and trim.** Continue wrapping the string across the roots while adding more sphagnum moss. Be sure all the roots are covered and trim the moss to shape.

6. **Secure the container**. Create holes on the back side of the small container and attach it to the driftwood or cork board with the two screws or nails. Make sure the wick is down in the container.

7. **Anchor the hanging hook behind the cork bark and hang.** Once your orchid display is hanging, fill the container with water to keep the moss and roots consistently moist.

Aftercare: I keep mine mounted on the wall with a small clip grow light attached to it. Maintenance is easy. Add water to the reservoir once a week and water the entire sphagnum moss ball every other week by dunking the whole thing in the sink. Depending on your light and environment, you may have to water more often or less. Keep the moss damp.

Moth orchids (*Phalaenopsis*), which are most commonly found at a local nursery, big box store, or plant shops, are epiphytic plants, meaning they naturally grow attached to other plants, like tree trunks and branches, rather than in soil. In nature, they take in moisture from the air, rain, and surrounding environment. In our homes, we grow orchids in pots and growing media to help retain moisture. Without any growing medium at all, they would need daily watering to stay hydrated.

DIY Trellis

You may find that adding a trellis is an easy way to change up the design of your plant display, instantly bringing new height, structure, and visual interest to your space. A trellis doesn't just elevate the look of a plant, but it also serves an important purpose for plants that naturally want to climb or attach themselves to something for support (hoyas, I'm talking to you!). Giving these plants a structure to grow on encourages healthier growth, fuller foliage, and more intentional direction rather than long, wandering vines.

The beauty of a DIY trellis is its simplicity. With just a couple of items, you can create something functional and stylish that fits your plant and your home aesthetic. Whether you prefer something minimal, sculptural, or playful, a handmade trellis allows you to customize the size, shape, and material to match your vision. It's a small project with a big impact.

materials you'll need:

- 9 gauge copper wire or a wire hanger
- Wire cutters
- Pot, bottle, or bowl (something to help form the shape)
- Plant clips or hook-and-loop plant tape to tie the plant to the trellis

1. **Cut the wire to size.** A good rule of thumb is to double the diameter of the pot. So if your pot is 5 inches (13 cm) wide, then your wire trellis will be 10 inches (25 cm) long. I would add a few more inches to the cut wire since you'll need to stick a portion of it into the soil to support itself.

2. **Shape the wire.** Tip! If your wire is extremely stiff and you have a drill, you can secure one end onto the drill and while holding the other end, twirl it slowly to make the wire a bit more moldable. Use the bowl or whatever item you're using to shape it into a hoop.

3. **Take your time!** Remember the shape doesn't have to be perfect! Once it's molded to your liking, bend the ends and insert them into the soil to form a ring.

4. **Attach the plant.** Secure the plant to the trellis by wrapping its vines or stems around it. To secure the stems in place, you can use plant tape or small claw clips.

7

Sharing the Joy of Plants

Plants have always been about connection. Long before social media, people shared what they grew. A neighbor handing down herbs from their kitchen window. Community gardeners sharing tips and tricks among themselves. A friend gifting a pothos cutting with roots just forming. A grandmother passing along her best advice to her grandchildren on how they care for their family's Christmas cactus and get it to bloom every year.

When you share a plant, you share *time.* You share *care.* You say "Here, this helped me. Maybe it'll help you too."

There's something magical that happens when you receive a plant as a gift. It's an instant boost of joy. Maybe it was a wish list plant and you can finally add it to your collection. Or perhaps you were given a propagated plant that has been in the giver's family for years. These plants tell a story and now that story continues in the comfort of your own collection.

I was gifted a 60-year-old philodendron (*Philodendron bipinnatifidum*) plant that grew so large that the owner unfortunately could no longer care for it anymore when they transitioned to a new home. No way that plant would fit in my mid-sized car, so with the help of my dad, we transported it with his Astro van. It was quite the adventure getting it home and repotted. I'm still recovering from that repot over a year later! I often wonder what this plant has seen and what stories it could tell if it had the ability to speak.

I mentioned earlier in the book that I have a Chinese evergreen plant (*Aglaonema* sp.) that was my late husband's favorite. Although he wasn't the biggest plant person, he named it Avatar and would check on it every chance he could. After he passed, I spent years trying to nurture it. It's still in my collection and sure, it's not as bushy as it once was, but those are the plants and the stories that stay close to our hearts. Plants build community and when you share plants, you're passing along joy, connections, and creating stories. In many ways, plant people speak their own language. We celebrate progress others might overlook. A new growth point. A bloom that lasted one more day than expected. A plant that survived a season we didn't think it would. Through plants, we learn to show up for one another with patience, curiosity, and grace, qualities that often spill into the rest of our lives.

Sharing Is Caring: Gifting a Piece of Growth

Plant gifting should be considered a love language. You brought that plant into your home, and you nurtured it with your joy, your energy, your patience. When you share them with someone else, you're offering a living symbol of those things all wrapped up into a beautiful vessel of foliage. That plant has a story and now you've passed it along so someone else can continue the story and enjoy the peace that plant provides in their

quick design tip

One of my favorite ways to share plant cuttings is by creating a flower frog out of clay or wire to support the cutting in its container (see page 152 for a DIY).

own life. That is the ultimate gift of love right there! You don't have to be elaborate to make plant-gifting meaningful. Even a simple cutting in a jar of water can become a symbol of care if offered with sincerity.

Here are some clever ways to find and share future plant buddies. They're all just one clip away!

- Take cuttings of favorite plants, put them in a "mystery propagation container" (see page 143) and pass it along to a friend.
- Host a plant swap or planty party.
- Set up a "take one, leave one" plant mailbox.
- Create a social media plant page.
- Start an online plant exchange.

Here are a few other thoughtful ways to gift plants

- Share propagation jars/containers with handwritten notes about how to care for the plant and where it came from. These help the new plant parent feel confident while preserving the story behind the cutting.
- Make plant gift baskets with soil, tools, and a baby plant. It's perfect for a beginner, offering everything they need to get started while removing the intimidation that often comes with first-time plant care.
- Have "just because" drop-offs for a neighbor, coworker, or friend who could use a little green magic, a simple reminder that care doesn't always need a reason, and that small, living gestures can brighten even the hardest days.

- Create a self-sustaining terrarium in a clear cookie jar that requires little to no maintenance for the plant lover in your life, offering them a tiny, living ecosystem that quietly thrives on its own. This gift is perfect for busy schedules, small spaces, or anyone who appreciates beauty without pressure. It basically takes care of itself with maybe just a few spritzes to the substrate when dry.
- Make the most of milestone gifts. How about gifting a money tree plant (*Pachira aquatica*) for birthdays, new jobs, graduations, or new homes? Traditionally associated with good fortune, prosperity, and positive energy, the money tree is believed to bring luck and abundance to the space it's grown in. Its braided trunk represents strength and interconnectedness, while its lush, hand-shaped leaves symbolize growth and opportunity.

below Plant gifting isn't just a trend; it's timeless. Whether it's a holiday, a housewarming, or a random Tuesday, giving someone a plant says, *I see you, and I want to bring a little life into your space.* Plants make especially powerful gifts during times of transition: new homes, new jobs, grief, healing, or fresh beginnings. They don't demand words when words feel heavy.

opposite A plant I'd especially recommend for a plant swap is the mistletoe cactus (*Rhipsalis baccifera*) with its long, thin, trailing stems spilling downward like a living waterfall of green. The plant's fine, grasslike segments create soft movement and texture, contrasting beautifully against any indoor background. The cuttings root easily and can be shared with others.

Plant Swaps and Green Gatherings

Hosting a plant swap is one of the most joyful, chaotic, and beautiful things a plant lover can do. You don't need to be an expert to host one. You just need a few friends, a table, and a spirit of sharing.

There's laughter, excitement over new plants, plant knowledge, and sometimes soil everywhere. More than that though, there's connection and potential to meet so many new plant friends.

Tips for a successful plant swap:

- Set a theme and determine the rules (i.e., propagations only, only rooted plants, harder to find plants, and so on).
- Have care tags available with plant identification and care advice so people know how to love their new green babies.
- Keep it casual and inclusive! No plant shaming allowed.

Beyond swaps, also consider:

- Hosting a "plant and sip" night
- Teaching a mini class in your community
- Playing a game of Plant Bingo
- Celebrate "Plantsgiving" during the holiday season—a time for you and other plant-loving friends to exchange plant-related items only. Plant accessories, plant cuttings, or wish list plant gifts.

Build a Plant Community

Need a reason for plant lovers to meet in a common place to learn about a plant topic? Yes, please! Here are two possible ideas to get started.

- Create a community garden or window herb-share in your neighborhood
- Create a social media plant page

As mentioned earlier, when I started my social media plant pages, it was simply to find other plant lovers to share the excitement of growing with. I didn't have anyone in my personal life who truly understood the desire to live in an indoor jungle or the chaos plant people willingly sign up for. Who else would understand making playlists "for the plants" because it just feels right? What about those spontaneous trips to a stranger's house to pick up a plant you spotted online? To some people, it might look like we've lost our marbles, but to plant people, it makes perfect sense. We absolutely get it.

There's something truly magical about finding common ground through plants. What starts as camaraderie over shared struggles, yellow leaves, surprise blooms, or failed propagations, slowly grows into genuine friendship. The friends I met through my plant page years ago have now become a meaningful part of my life, and our relationship has grown far beyond

a case of awkward turned amazing

I have had the amazing opportunity to meet so many of you through the years and the hysterical interactions we've shared always make me chuckle. Mind you, I am one person creating content in her home and rambling about plants, so to actually physically see that there are real people behind the screens is still mind-boggling to me. The first time I met one of you in person—oh, it was absolutely terrible. Not because of the other person (she was so kind and I am so grateful for the grace she showed me), but because I didn't know what to say. She came up to me to tell me how much she appreciated my content, and while I was overjoyed, I instantly got painfully shy. I said hi . . . and basically ran away. My mom was with me at the time, and even she tells me how awkward I was. If you're reading this—I'm so sorry! I promise it's better now. After years of practice, the shyness has mostly faded, replaced with something much sweeter—genuine connection. Every conversation, hug, laugh, and shared plant story has helped me realize that this community isn't just about plants; it's about people. Anytime I hear someone yell out "chunky soil mix" or whisper "Drown that hoe" as we've walked past each other, you've turned something I started alone into something deeply shared. And I don't take that lightly. Each interaction, no matter how brief, I'm so grateful. Awkward moments and all.

try this

Every time you propagate a plant, label it with the story of where it came from and challenge the recipient to pass it on again whenever they can.

screens and comments. If it weren't for plants, and the courage to share that love online, our paths would have never crossed. Plants became the bridge and an easy entry point into deeper long-term connection.

Book That Plant Trip, and If You Have No One to Go With, Go Solo!

I have to tell you this story. I promise it ties into the chapter, so bear with me, but this plant adventure felt monumental. It's one of those *you are where you're supposed to be* moments that stays with you long after it's over. As I've navigated this stage

Stapelia gigantea is a succulent that has star-shaped, pale yellow- to cream-colored flowers, covered in reddish hairs and dramatic veining. These out-of-this-world-looking flowers emit a strong odor of rotting flesh. This scent attracts its natural pollinators, flies. While shocking, the smell usually only lasts a few days and is strongest when the flower is fully open.

of my life as a onesome, I've intentionally pushed myself outside of my comfort zone. One of the biggest ways I've done that is through solo travel.

In my Latino family, solo traveling is not really a thing. It's often viewed as unusual, almost concerning, that someone would want to go somewhere alone. And after being married for so long, it wasn't something I ever did. Traveling was always a shared experience. But in this new chapter of my life, I've come to understand just how short and unpredictable life truly is. I no longer want to wait for the "right time" or the "right person" to experience it with. I don't want to stop living fully just because I couldn't find someone else to go with me. Life can carry deep hurt and pain, but it is also overflowing with beauty and I made a decision to keep searching for it, even when doing so felt uncomfortable. Over the years, social media has introduced me to incredible people, and a few years ago, a group of us began meeting up for plant adventures at events in different states. Those trips were special, but this one was different. This was my first truly spontaneous plant trip; one I took alone, just for me.

I naturally have gravitated toward the weirder plants through the years but not just weird, the smelly ones too! The carrion plant *(Stapelia gigantea)*, with its massive blooms that smell like rotting flesh, is absolutely in my top five favorite stinky bloomers. Over the years of searching for one to own, I finally purchased the one I now have in my collection.

I found a konjac plant (*Amorphophallus konjac*) at my local nursery and fell in love with the tenacity of the bloom, her stunning burgundy color, and yes, her odor. She's another stinky one and more stinky than the *Stapelia*. It bloomed in my home for the first time and, let me tell you something, the smell carried throughout my entire top floor. So much so, I had to close her in a room so I could sleep without the smell keeping me

The konjac plant has a transformative growth cycle. When it's not in its bloom phase (the bloom phase is when it smells horribly) it is in its leaf phase, shown here. The plant sends up a single enormous leaf that looks like a small tree. This phase can last many months while the plant photosynthesizes to build energy for continued growth. Once the leaf dies back, the corm underneath the soil goes dormant until it is ready to regrow.

Moment checked off my planty bucket list! I captured the exact moment I was able to see and smell the *Amorphophallus titanum* at the Missouri Botanical Garden. I'm not sure how many people have this on their list of things to do, but if it's not on your list, add it right now.

up at night. My goodness though, she is beautiful and so interesting to learn about.

With my love for smelly plants, I made it my mission to visit one of the smelliest and largest blooms in the world, the titan arum (a.k.a. the corpse flower) (*Amorphophallus titanum*). What makes this *Amorphophallus* so special, other than its smell, is how quickly the bloom fades. The smell brings its pollinators with the stench of rotten meat, but that flower only blooms for a few days. The kicker is it can take five to seven years, sometimes even longer, for the plant to mature enough to bloom. Catching it open and in action front and center is something that thousands of people go searching for—and line up to smell—at botanical gardens. On this newfound journey of solo adventures, I came across two botanical gardens that had a titan arum on the verge of blooming, so I made the spontaneous decision to visit. Alone. I had to time this correctly because, like I mentioned, there's no real way of knowing when the flower would open and be in its stinkiest form. I decided that instead of trying to time the opening and having to catch a flight to California to visit The Huntington Botanical Gardens, I would go to the Missouri Botanical Garden (MBG) instead, which is about four hours away from me, and take the chance.

I can't even begin to describe the euphoria that navigated my body as I drove four hours to see the titan arum. It felt like I was chasing a once-in-a-lifetime moment, and a whole lot of anticipation coursed through me. As I shared this adventure on social media, it was compared to when a mother is preparing to give birth: the excitement of knowing something incredible is coming, paired with the anxiety of timing it just right. That comparison couldn't have been more accurate.

I arrived at the MBG on Thursday, and unfortunately the flower was still tightly closed, no movement yet. I explored the area on Friday. Still no movement from our friend. I knew that if by Saturday night, no changes were made, I would miss it since I had to be back on the road by Sunday morning. I checked the live stream on Saturday afternoon and holy smokes, there she was! It was the evening before I was set to leave and she was opening! I was exactly at the place I was supposed to be and at the right time. They opened up MBG that evening and stayed open overnight for anyone who wanted to witness this grand event. The line formed to see her was so long. I couldn't believe how many people were this excited to see it too. At 11 p.m., I got to check something off my plant bucket list. I got to see *and smell* this beauty! Did it smell as bad as they said it would? It absolutely did. It also radiates heat, so the warmth and the intertwining of rotten carcass smell is pretty nasty. It's a moment I'll never forget.

Why this story is important to share is because some of these experiences have not felt natural to me. I *love* being home and surrounded by my own plants. I have had to push through those feelings of uncertainty, those feelings of uncomfortableness, the anxiety of new experiences, but because of my passion for plants, I've been able to push myself through my own fears.

Plants have been my bridge through those moments. They've given me a reason to say yes when fear told me to stay still. They've pulled me into rooms full of strangers who instantly felt familiar because we were all there for the same reason—the love of plants. Passion has a way of shrinking fear, and plants have continually reminded me that curiosity is stronger than hesitation.

Wherever you are in your plant journey, I hope you find a space amongst the green that clears the mind in seasons of loss, change, or loneliness. A place where tending to something living also becomes a quiet act of care for yourself. Let it serve as a reminder that we are allowed to seek joy, even in moments that feel heavy. Sometimes joy can be small, like a new leaf unfurling, a cutting taking root, or the peace found in sitting still among plants as they silently grow. Whatever life has in store for you, continue to hold plants close to your heart and as always, *keep on growing*.

If you ever need grounding, go where things are growing.

Acknowledgments

This book would not exist without the love, encouragement, and belief of so many people who have shaped me both in life and along this journey.

To my parents: Thank you for giving me roots strong enough to grow and wings brave enough to explore. You taught me patience, resilience, and the importance of showing up consistently, even when progress felt slow or uncertain. Your belief in me never stopped, even when I believed I didn't have it in me to continue. Through your actions, you taught me the value of hard work, compassion, and integrity. You two are my foundation, my rock, and my reminder of where I come from, and I couldn't have accomplished this dream without you both. My viejitos, I love you.

To my community of plant lovers and friends I've met through this shared love of plants: Thank you for trusting me, learning alongside me, and reminding me every day of why I love this space. Your messages, stories, questions, and encouragement turned a personal passion into a shared experience. You showed me that plants connect us in ways far deeper than having an indoor jungle. They connect us to patience, healing, and each other. I am forever appreciative for your support every single day.

For the team at Quarto Publishing and Cool Springs Press: Thank you for your expertise and guidance throughout the development

of this book. Oh my gosh, I can't believe I wrote a whole book! Thank you for believing in this book and in my voice. Your support helped transform an idea and a dream of mine into something tangible and meaningful. It has been an honor to work alongside people who supported me through this vision, and trusted in it to truly thrive.

To my photographer, Kat Schleicher: Thank you for capturing the heart of this book through your lens. Your images bring these pages to life and reflect the warmth and intention behind every plant and moment. This book would not feel the same without your artistry.

To Bennett's Greenhouse: Thank you for generously allowing me to photograph within your space and for welcoming me so openly among the plants. During times when I needed quiet, grounding, and a place to breathe, your nursery became an escape. It offered comfort, clarity, and so many new plants. I'm grateful for the role it played in both this book and my journey.

For my late husband: Your love remains with me, in the way I care, the way I grow, and the way I continue forward. I wish you were here to see it, but you are part of every chapter, even the ones written after loss.

I'll carry you with me, always.

And finally, to the plants themselves: Thank you for teaching me how to slow down, pay attention, and grow with intention . . . except for those stubborn chia seeds and the dramatic fiddle leaf fig: You made my life more stressful than it needed to be, but I had a lot of fun trying to grow you.

Always remember to keep on growing,

—Krystal

About the Author

Krystal Duran is the creator behind PlantswithKrystal. She is a dedicated plant educator, content creator, and entrepreneur with a mission to make plant care accessible, engaging, and rewarding. With over ten years of hands-on experience, she has built a trusted brand that blends expert knowledge with a personal, relatable approach. Through her content, she has empowered plant enthusiasts to cultivate thriving green spaces, whether in their homes or through larger botanical projects.

Follow along with Krystal's adventures on:
Instagram: @_plantswithkrystal_
TikTok: @plantswithkrystal
Facebook: facebook.com/plantswithkrystal
YouTube: @plantswithkrystal
On the web: www.plants-with-krystal.com

Index

R

S

Krystal